R E L I G I O N

RELIGION

Rereading What Is Bound Together

MICHEL SERRES

Translated by Malcolm DeBevoise

STANFORD UNIVERSITY PRESS
Stanford, California

STANFORD UNIVERSITY PRESS
Stanford, California

Religion was originally published in French in 2019 under the title *Relire le relié*, by Michel Serres © Editions Le Pommier/ Humensis, 2019

Printed in the United States of America on acid-free, archival-quality paper

Library of Congress Cataloging-in-Publication Data

Names: Serres, Michel, author. | DeBevoise, M. B., translator.
Title: Religion : rereading what is bound together / Michel Serres ; translated by Malcolm DeBevoise.
Other titles: Relire le relié. English
Description: Stanford, California : Stanford University Press, 2022. | "Originally published in French in 2019 under the title Relire le relié." | Includes bibliographical references and index.
Identifiers: LCCN 2021050003 (print) | LCCN 2021050004 (ebook) | ISBN 9781503628755 (cloth) | ISBN 9781503631496 (paperback) | ISBN 9781503631502 (epub)
Subjects: LCSH: Religion—Philosophy. | Violence—Philosophy. | Good and evil—Philosophy.
Classification: LCC BL51 .S469713 2022 (print) | LCC BL51 (ebook) | DDC 210—dc23/eng/20211201
LC record available at https://lccn.loc.gov/2021050003
LC ebook record available at https://lccn.loc.gov/2021050004

Cover design: Rob Ehle, Kevin Barrett Kane

Cover image: Vittore Carpaccio, *St. Augustine in His Studio*, 1502, 56" × 83", tempera on panel

Text design: Kevin Barrett Kane

Typeset at Stanford University Press in 11/15 ITC Galliard Pro

for MARIE-LAURE DURAND,
a promise is a promise

with gratitude and affection
To Suzanne,
model of saintliness

CONTENTS

A NOTE ON THE TRANSLATION

Michel Serres was working as fast as he could in order to deliver a finished manuscript, in the event only a day before he died, and so did not have an opportunity to correct page proof. The French edition, printed directly from the files received from the author, is marred by infelicities of various kinds that no doubt he would have wished to eliminate. In making an English translation, I have made every effort to ensure that silent modifications of the text, additions and subtractions alike, are consonant not only with the sense and spirit of the French but also with the thrust of Serres's work as a whole, and especially the attempts at synthesis over the last two decades. The subject of this final book, religion, plainly preoccupied him throughout his life.

I have streamlined the table of contents for the sake of clarity and consistency, seeking to bring out the main theme of each chapter. The various subsidiary themes—involving the idea of hot spots, networks (or webs) of relations, false

gods, love and death in relation to violence, and so forth—
frequently recur in the section titles, and no reader will fail
either to understand their importance or to grasp their connection with one another.

MALCOLM DEBEVOISE

PREFACE

Then the scribes and Pharisees brought [to Jesus] a woman who had been caught in adultery, and placing her in the midst they said to him, "Teacher, this woman has been caught in the act of adultery. Now, in the law, Moses commanded that such should be stoned. What do you say?" . . . But Jesus bent down and wrote with his finger on the ground [as though he did not hear]. And as they continued to ask him, he stood up and said to them, "Let him who is without sin among you be the first to throw a stone at her." And once more he bent down and wrote with his finger on the ground.

John 8:3–8

As it was well understood by men that the woman alone had committed adultery, an agreement was reached among them that she should be stoned. Violence within a group was focused on an individual. This human sacrifice may be said to have *bound together* the murderers.

Before responding and pardoning, Jesus bent down to write on the ground. As if the evangelist, in his account, had pointed to a passage written beneath his own, in Jesus's hand, just as a palimpsest displays one script and hides another. Must we reread the one in order to decipher the other?

Linguists tell us that the term "religion" has two sources, one more probable than the other: *rereading* and *binding together*. In what follows, by ceaselessly *reading* texts in the hope of being able to *reread* the very one that Jesus wrote down on the ground, I try to place the two meanings in perspective, as Saint John the Apostle's account does here. Must we *read* it as saying that, in pardoning the victim, without punishing her executioners, it *undoes* the agreement that *binds together* these men in infamy? This is the question that the present book seeks to answer.

RELIGION

CHAPTER 1

VERTICAL BINDING

Earth and Heaven

Ever since a benevolent teacher initiated me into the mystery of the unknown x, and, in doing this, introduced me to mathematical abstraction, ever since he taught me its many and often incredible practical applications, I have believed in the existence of a virtual world—invisible, formal, and, what is more, multiply layered—since later I found it in various forms, not only in law, medicine, and the fine arts, but also in private and public life. I should not say merely that I believe in this virtual world: I see it, like everyone else; what is more, I have lived a part of my life in it, I have immersed myself in it.

I begin with mathematics because those who are strangers to its sublime beauties have a harder time perceiving this virtual world than those who, in grappling with mathematics, have run up against its stubborn resistance, its proud independence, and understood its real utility. The virtual world does not submit to our laws; quite to the contrary, we obey its laws, which are discovered rather than invented, and which give access to the laws of the physical world—the same laws, miraculously, as those of mathematics.

How could we survive without this absent world that shapes our innermost being, that inflames our imaginations, that shapes our relations with others, both individually and collectively, that enriches human perception—this world whose notoriously unreasonable effectiveness alleviates the sorrows of life and lightens the burdens of work? Is it too much to claim that our deliberate use of mathematics for so many purposes sets us apart from our animal cousins? To claim that our essence and virtue as human beings reside in our manipulation of this virtual world, whose subtle gradations call to mind the color spectrum, with all its infinitely fine shades?

Once our ancestors began to paint animals and signs on the walls of caves, which is to say once they invented representation (the very term indicates the difference between absence and presence: this is not an animal, and so on); once they began, in Malta, for example, some forty thousand years ago in the Upper Paleolithic, to sculpt an improbable man-lion, with two-bodied gods of good fortune later migrating more or less everywhere, from Egypt to Mexico, another world emerged, mythical, alien, formal, imaginary, aesthetic, symbolic—I do not know how to characterize it, except to say that it is a world different from the one our immediate sensations reveal, a world that no less surely constrains our freedom of maneuver. And with the advent of spoken language, the reference and meaning of words marked out the intersection between the world we live in and categories external to it.

Plastic, supple, fluent, labile, sometimes as dense and transparent as a diamond, this other world manifests itself in different ways, depending on the place, that unfold in the form of histories. The majority of living species display roughly analogous behaviors at all latitudes, whereas human cultures, languages, religions, conventions, contractual arrangements, and the like are liable to differ markedly over small distances and in similar climates. And yet each culture evolves in such a way that successive generations of a single group may differ from one another no less than neighboring peoples differ from one another. Thus culture takes over from nature by means of a sort of exo-Darwinism in which mutations and selection occur more quickly and with greater adaptive capacity than biological evolution itself. When spring arrives we take off our warm clothes in far less time than it takes for an animal to shed its coat. The formal world conditions how we perceive our own world and permits us to make it a more hospitable habitat, better suited to our needs.

The Hearth in Which a Log Burns

Question: Is the spiritual world evoked by religion just one among many others, or does it show—does it form, I should say, by virtue of its distribution over all cultures and of its temporal antiquity—the trunk from which these other worlds branch off, the burning source of all the rest that subsequently cools? I am sometimes inclined to favor the latter alternative, for if these other worlds often shine like light on a translucent ice floe, the religious world not only shines, it burns with intense brilliance: light and energy both, of that there can be no doubt. Nevertheless some other virtual worlds are liable also to catch fire and then to start similar fires in their turn. The fertile heat of the religious flame brings forth much that is new, but sometimes only at the cost of appalling violence. A holy flame, to be sure, but a sacred one as well, a flame that encourages innumerable murderous sacrifices. If it did not burn so fiercely, religions would not have been able to recruit so many followers; from such inauspicious beginnings, they would not have been able to flourish for thousands of years. I do not know if this hypothesis is true; in fact I often suspect it is not. Even so, comparing various virtual worlds is well worth the effort, as I will now attempt to show.

The Other World

Proofs that virtual worlds exist are to be found everywhere. Mathematical techniques—invisible and absent, but nonetheless inevitable—can decipher anything. How is that we can give meaning to signals that are propagated by waves? Where does the trust that we place in contracts come from? Why do we live so often in our imaginations, filled with dreams, memories of the past, and hopes for the future? Would our world exist, the one we know as human beings, without the mathematical world, since without this other world we would not be able to understand our own and make it livable? Equations and algorithms, triangles and polyhedrons, language and music, musical notation and alphabets, images—where are all these things to be found? Show me their place and their home.

But this other world, abstract, virtual, possible, whatever else it may be, sometimes manifests its existence in our world by suddenly emerging in places of exceptional heat that, once they have cooled, are so long-lasting that their traces lie outside the boundaries of historical time. Let us call them "hot spots."

Fire

We now know how to detect the places where fire beneath the earth's tectonic plates, here and there more intense than elsewhere, pierces them and causes volcanic eruptions similar to those that occur on the islands of Réunion and Hawaii, or leaves behind cooled remains, like the Maldives or the Deccan Traps in west central India.

Similarly, we have mapped the various places where meteorites have struck the earth, from Siberia to the Yucatán peninsula of Mexico. There the cosmos and the netherworld abruptly came into contact with the surface of our planet, causing it to burst into flames and spew lava, masses of molten rock, and clouds. In the extreme case the result may be equivalent to a nuclear winter. Light and darkness, creative and destructive energy—in this case violent energy.

By analogy, then, I call "hot spots" those places where, at a given moment, another world manifests itself in ours, those concrete images of contact with another reality, be it virtual, intelligent, spiritual, inspirational—perhaps dangerous as well.

Building a Barrier

Our Latin ancestors imagined that Jupiter, seated in his high Olympus, hurled down thunderbolts when he was angered. The Gauls, we are told, also dreaded this unforeseeable barrage. The Romans surrounded the place where lightning struck with a low wall of stone and bronze known as a *puteal* (from the Latin *puteus*) for its resemblance to a wellhead. Now, if a well puts a subterranean source into communication with the earth's surface, a *puteal* marked the spot where heaven and earth came together in a blazing short circuit. Did those who constructed this barrier around the

spot where lightning had struck fear that this spot diffused
a lethal energy, like a star?

The word *puteus* meant both well and chimney, two vertical relations in one, fiery and aqueous, up and down, between
another world and this one—earth beneath our feet, fire above
in the heavens, water risen up from the depths. As for air,
the word that designates the soul, invisible and incorporeal,
expresses its animate character through the act of breathing.
Are other worlds composed of the same elements as ours?

Tales of Water

One evening a girl named Rebecca was drawing water from a
well for her family's meal and for their animals, as she did every
evening, when Isaac appeared in the form of an intermediary,
his servant, a traveler parched with thirst. Another girl, named
Rachel, was likewise drawing water at a wellhead when Jacob
appeared, thirsty as well. Each one drank from the pitcher
that the girl offered him; each one took the girl who offered
him water as his wife. From the love radiated by these wells
there came a posterity as dense as the crown of a beech tree.

Many generations later, in the same fashion, a Samaritan
woman met the Son of Man at another such wellhead. Jesus
said to her: our ancestors drank this water and died; I will
give you to drink the water of eternal life. From this well,
in which water was transubstantiated into ambrosia, there
radiated the resurrection of the dead.

Tales of Fire

The projected shadow of the sundial was useful less as a way
of telling time, something to which our ancestors attached
little importance, than of observing the relation between
heavenly phenomena and a particular state of affairs on earth.

To this, for example, we owe the invention of the latitude scale. The sundial therefore functioned less as a clock than as an astronomical observatory. The vertical axis intercepting sunlight—which is to say the part of the sundial that casts a shadow, the shaft (or pointer)—the Greeks called *gnomon*, a word that in their language meant knowing, understanding. Was this the first lightning rod?

Here we have not one but two blazing short circuits: between the sun and the ground by light and shadow, as our eyes see it, but above all between a vertical, material shaft and a decodable knowledge, as I like to call computer software; between the concrete, on the one hand, and the abstract, on the other; between the energy of light and the subtlety of information. A hot spot, in other words.

From this relation between light and shadow it was possible to acquire information about space and time on earth. Here we have one of the first realizations of an artificial intelligence: a metal shaft is said to be *gnomon*, that is, knowing. The sun came down to earth and, with its shadow, wrote on it marks, a kind of script, that had to be decoded. Thus the energy of the solar fire brought forth information.

The Sun's Fire in the Pyramid
Thales is said to have invented his theorem by comparing the shadow cast by one of the three great pyramids of Egypt with the one cast at the same hour by a man. This gnomonic story, as it might well be called, omits to note that anyone standing at the foot of Khufu, not merely Thales, could have seen that Khafre and Menkaure are similar figures. The theory of homothetic forms, which is to say figures having the same form but on different scales, is illustrated here in visible, tangible stones. Sundials, the story says. Objection: no matter

that the height of a man and the length of the shadows cast
by his upright body and the shaft (or *gnomon*) of a sundial
were easily measured, the line that went to the exact center of
the pyramid remained hidden beneath a thick wall of stone.

To make the line visible, it was necessary to conceive of
an abstract volume, the tetrahedron—empty, luminous, and
transparent; that is, the sun had to be brought into the very
darkness of this edifice. Geometry therefore did not come
into being solely by means of a gnomonic representation of
light and shadow; it was also revealed in a wholly different
manner, at the moment when the sun descended into a blind
mass and penetrated it. Can we begin to imagine how much
solar energy was needed to chase opacity from the stone?

Here, in a way that is readily visualized, we apprehend
the dazzling discovery of the abstract. At the foot of Khufu,
Thales contemplated a blinding short circuit between this
world and another one: the sudden intuition of homothetic-
ity and the black box of stone pierced by the light of the
sun, as though it were lightning. It was for this reason that
the Greeks named the structure "pyramid," which is to say
fire; and when Plato, in the *Timaeus*, describes the parallel
between earthly elements and abstract polyhedrons, he associates fire with the tetrahedron, which is to say with the
pyramid: fire comes down to earth and enters it. In order
to invent geometry, by means of a theorem that retains its
validity still today, after thousands of years, was it therefore
necessary to surround a hot spot with a puteal?

Plato goes on later in the *Timaeus* to say that physical
measurement, because it is always approximate, can never
attain the ideal precision of geometry, unlike stereometry,
the measurement of regular polyhedrons, which he was the

first to reduce to five basic types. A sun must have penetrated and emptied these black volumes!

Water and Fire Again

Another Greek legend relates the drowning of Hippasus of Metapontum, accused by the Pythagoreans of having divulged the secret, nervously guarded by the members of the brotherhood, concerning the discovery, shameful but inevitable, of irrational lengths and numbers whose infinite extension destroyed the serenity of *logos*, reason, and proportion. Are we to interpret Hippasus's drowning at sea— precisely the bottomless well that we met with earlier—as a divine punishment or as a sort of collective lynching?

Yet another legend tells of Archimedes's use of mirrors to set fire to the Roman fleet besieging Syracuse in the third century BCE by reflecting the rays of the sun. Here, with literally lightning suddenness, we pass from geometrical optics to combats in which soldiers, now transformed into torches, are killed; from *gnomon* to massacre. Information is returned to energy, energy assumes the form of violence.

Traveling around the island of Sicily we encounter next Empedocles, one of the earliest physicists, who, again according to legend, committed suicide by throwing himself into the crater of Etna, and then Ettore Majorana, who more than twenty centuries later mysteriously disappeared, no one knows why, though no doubt he was frightened at having come into possession, at least from a distance, of the quasi-solar fires of the atomic bomb. In this case we pass from physics to massive destruction, from an inventive puteal to a destructive one, from the abstract to the concrete, from information to energy, and finally to violence: volcano, incendiary mirrors, the lucid and blind announcement of Hiroshima . . .

If the triangular island of Sicily, a scale model of our world and its history, displays three local hot spots, it may well be wondered whether today we are transforming our world into a global hot spot. We have long believed that the fires of science produce less violence than those of religion. We were mistaken.

Mathematical Physics

Contrary to a persistent legend, neither Copernicus nor Galileo managed to establish the reality of heliocentrism, limited as they were by the relativity of motions. Pascal, Descartes, and Leibniz rightly reaffirmed the equivalence of their theories, asserted long before by ancient Greek astronomers. It was not until 1725, however, when James Bradley discovered the aberration of light, that the sun was actually shown to be at the center of the planetary system. Then and only then was Kant able to speak of a "Copernican revolution," thus setting truth on the retrograde course from which the legend arose.

Galileo's true originality, which was to prove decisive, has to do with the connection he established between mathematics and experiment. The Greeks had missed this point of intersection, with the result that they were unable to develop an exact science of the world. Galileo, by associating a particular equation with a particular experiment, succeeded in creating a blindingly fruitful short circuit between a formal, virtual world and the real world that we perceive. In so doing, he heralded the advent of modern science. His method uncovered a hot spot.

The philosopher of science Alexandre Kojève grasped what was really at stake in Galileo's famous trial. Galileo invented mathematical physics, which is to say he brought a concrete experiment carried out in this world into contact with an equation that had been known for centuries, suspended in a virtual world, pure and abstract. His invention, which Einstein called a miracle and which I call a hot spot, showed that only mathematics, however formal, virtual, and absent it may be, is capable of decoding reality, of writing the great book of nature, as Galileo put it, in its own language.

Now, the Church of Rome taught the Incarnation of Jesus Christ, which is to say a short circuit, blindingly luminous and charged with a unique truth, between the real, incarnate world, on the one hand, and, on the other, a kingdom utterly separate from it—a hot spot, if ever there was one. Did Galileo discredit the doctrine that the earth is at the center of the universe by an analogous gesture? Did the importance of his trial derive from a similarity between this dogmatic puteal and the short circuit brought about by mathematical physics? Were these two hot spots, these two points of contact between the immanent and the transcendent, unforeseeable and unimaginable, themselves somehow related?

The universe of physical laws involves all of mathematics—geometry, topology, algebra, number theory and algorithms, probability calculus, and so on. The plurality of these laws traces a sort of silhouette of mathematics as a whole. Scientific discovery therefore creates a direct link between a precise locality in the realm of mathematics and a definite phenomenon of the real world, a thread of the fabric that, virtually at least, unites equations and experiments. Thus a short circuit produces another hot spot.

Kojève suspected that mathematical physics emerged—perhaps could only have emerged—in the context of the doctrine of the Incarnation. Pascal had the same intuition in connection with his search for a fixed point: no learning, not even the most rigorous, could furnish such a point; only Jesus Christ himself, the central body to which everything tends, could supply it. The totality of the sciences turns around this sun.

That there exists another world than ours should therefore be plain; that one should turn out to be older than all the others in no way proves that it is the cause of them, their stock or trunk—*post hoc sed non propter hoc.*

Three Questions

The things we manipulate, the ideas we form, the organizations we establish—can they be seen as more or less distantly or recently cooled formations arising from an underlying furnace? As pozzolana of variable profiles and size, swirling clouds of dust, massive and deformed bombs, all of them concretions issued from a primitive fire, either subterranean and permanent or, more rarely, celestial, in which case they assume the form of aerolites, stony meteors falling to earth, landing here and there? How can we describe these furnaces, if not as being religious in nature?

Two Limiting Cases

First, an individual example. The mystic burns with an inner fire, a divine fire that he internalizes, a Promethean fire brought down to earth, a fire that creates and illuminates—thus God brought forth, then and there, amidst the fantastic heat of a primitive nebula, a tremendous big bang of energy that incited mystics to undertake admirable things, but whose intense flame burned heretics and witches and provoked horrible conflicts. We live between two fires: the one spread by the sun and the stars throughout space, the other submerged in the chthonic depths, one becoming heaven, the other hell. Recall once again Empedocles, author of the dual law of hatred and love, said to have leapt into Etna's crater, a very hot spot indeed.

Next, collective examples, in the form of another series of questions. How does politics emerge from this fire? Does *temporal* power mobilize *energy on the entropic scale*, energy that is powerful and deadly: hierarchies, violence, wars, all so frequent that they dominate history; whereas so-called *spiritual* power removes *information* from history, information that is subtle and exceedingly rare?

Do the ideas of nation and fatherland—the one no less formal and sublime than the other, capable of *binding together* crowds, by demanding that each participant give his life to them—do they really differ from imaginary goddesses and gods who cruelly unleash enthusiasm and require martyrdom? The same hot source in each case, but concretions so different that one hesitates to compare them.

How did religions themselves emerge from this fire? By separating the temporal cardinals from the cloistered, spiritual, and mystic nuns and monks. And the sciences? By setting ministers and rectors apart from researchers, solitary inventors. In each case energy flanked by entropy, on the one hand, and, on the other, information, subtle, rare, silent, inaudible.

Fathoming the depths of these hot spots, piercing the impenetrable thickness of myths so dark that we are shocked to find ourselves enlightened by them, attempting to understand this strange process of crystallization—thus my mad hope in this book.

Two Myths

Let us now look at two myths of this type, ancient legends. Midas, king of Phrygia, was said to have received from

Dionysus the power of transforming everything he touched into gold. But he soon regretted this miraculous gift, since food and drink turned into metal in his hands and between his lips before he could consume them. Wracked by hunger and thirst, in danger of dying, he implored the god to deprive him of his new ability. Dionysus ordered him to cleanse himself at the source of the river Patolus, in the neighboring country of Lydia. Following this royal immersion the river carried off nuggets of gold, forming the rich alluvial deposits for which it was known in ancient times.

Gyges was a shepherd employed by the king of Lydia. One day he lost a sheep. Leaving the herd, he wandered in the countryside, searching for the missing animal. On coming to the foot of a rock face, he found that an earthquake had opened up a cave; on going inside, and descending through a sort of well, he came to a tomb containing a naked recumbent figure, a former king, who wore a gold ring on his middle finger. Gyges took it for himself and went on his way; we do not know whether he found his sheep. Later, while conversing with other shepherds, he distractedly rubbed the gem set in the ring and miraculously became invisible. This allowed him to enter the royal palace unseen, seduce the queen and kill the king, and so to seize the crown. Thus the king's shepherd became king himself. Croesus, the richest of all ancient kings, was the last to reign over Lydia.

Mere myths, these two legends?

A First Thunderbolt

The legendary lives and deeds of Midas, Gyges, and Croesus are our earliest evidence, subsequently affirmed by tradition and confirmed by archeology, that money appeared for the first time in Lydia around the seventh century BCE. A

brilliant invention since henceforth, whether through pur-
chase, sale, or exchange, everything could be transformed
into gold and silver—what Marx called the money form of
value, the universal equivalent. And all the more brilliant as
the hidden, almost invisible power of money allowed anyone
possessing it to interfere in all places and undertakings, to
take advantage of princesses and to seize power in all its many
forms for himself. Money as the Midas of metamorphosis and
the Gyges of invisibility: thus its two virtual virtues; thus how
to *reread* its double *legend*.

Not far from Lydia, in Miletus, at about the same time,
in 625, Thales was born, the mathematician who, according
to a similar tradition, discovered geometry. Later, a little to
the south, in Cnidus, Eudoxus invented the rudiments of
algebra; a little to the north, on the island of Samos, Pythagoras was born, he of the eponymous theorem. Renan
called these immortal inventions the "Greek miracle." Quite
near to Cnidus, on the island of Cos, Hippocrates was born,
around the middle of the fifth century, the physician whom
tradition credits with having transformed medical practice
into a rational science.

In the same region, from the thirteenth to the seventh
centuries, Phoenicians and Greeks, starting from hundreds
of abstract symbols, had little by little created a rudimentary
alphabet consisting of some three or four dozen characters,
which became the letters of the Greek, Roman, Hebrew,
Arabic, and Cyrillic scripts. These innovations, arbitrary and
formal though they were, yet managed to designate all the
things of the world.

A single groundswell, of whose origin we are ignorant
but whose energy and scale we can only admire, led cultures
that flourished in Ionia during the last millennium before

the Common Era to introduce money, mathematics, and a
basic writing system. Here three virtual worlds came to be
realized and, with them, the trust underlying commercial
exchange, the ideal forms of geometry, and linguistic conventions. Would we, descendants of this ancient civilization, be
able to go forward without these treasures, so alike that they
are seldom compared and their common emergence seldom
recognized? From what deep-seated energy source did these
forms of information burst forth into our world?

Universal Equivalence

What did these three discoveries have in common? Equipped
with gold and silver, in short, with money, you can buy, sell,
or exchange food, clothes, lodging, labor of various kinds,
and much else—a very long list that covers almost all our
needs and desires. Money, the universal equivalent, is worth
everything and anything, even though in itself it is worth
nothing. It is everywhere present and invisible, virtual and
yet at every instant actual. Thus the virtual descends to the
actual, now transformed by abstraction.

The same is true for algebraic terms and geometrical
forms: the circle, which does not exist, allows you to express
everything in the world that is round; the unknown x, which
by itself has no value, can assume all values. Likewise, a letter,
meaningless by itself, takes on almost any meaning whatever
depending on the place it occupies in a word or a sentence.

Money, the x of algebra, and the letters of the alphabet,
though they have no meaning, can have all meanings. In
each of these three cases, abstraction and the virtual turn out
always to be applicable to the concrete: to what one wishes
to sell, exchange, or buy; to what one wishes to understand
or undertake; to what one wishes to say or write. Is there a

more decisive moment in history than the one that marks these three roughly contemporaneous births? Three hot spots, once again, next to the sea, itself volcanic.

An Even Bigger Thunderbolt

Alongside this upheaval, another one gathered strength whose consequences were to be still more momentous. Within the space of a few decades, as Karl Jaspers noted, in the same millennium and almost the same century, a giant tsunami traveled across the whole of Eurasia and brought forth there almost all the great religious movements, based on the teaching of wise men: Confucius and Laozi in China, Buddha in India, Zoroaster in Persia, Abraham and monotheism in Israel, and finally the pre-Socratic Greek philosophers, who were also geometers. I am quite prepared to compare this tidal wave of hot spots with the line of geophysical eruptions that occurred either horizontally, in the Pacific, throughout the Hawaiian islands, or, more vertically, in the Indian Ocean, from Réunion to the Deccan plateau in India. Still today there is much disagreement over exact dates, but together they form a crucial period in human history that Jaspers called the axial age, because it provides a temporal axis that can serve as a stable point of reference for the quite varied set of civilizations and cultures that covered both Europe and Asia like an immense mosaic.

Did the tidal wave that brought about the birth of mathematics, money, and the alphabet in a relatively limited area of Europe and Asia Minor bear any relation to the one that caused the major religions to appear over the whole of the Eurasian continent? Can they be seen as two components of a single seismic wave of surpassing intensity that profoundly shook this part of earth? The discoveries of money, mathematics, and the alphabet, soon all but crystalized, with only small variations over time, gave rise to histories as long-lasting and stable as those of religions, whose constancy and duration far exceed what one finds in the case of historical empires, all the more fragile as their power is great.

Ever since then humanity has sought not only to explain and dominate the world, but also to understand itself, by means of four networks, or webs of relations: money, science, language, and religion. Languages subdivide into dialects, accents, local expressions, technical vocabularies, and so on; money is found throughout the world in the guise of different currencies, nearly as many as there are countries; the sciences are broken down into disciplines and specialties, religions into churches, rites, sects, orthodoxies and heresies. The subdivisions are similar.

All cultures are steeped in religion, as ethnology amply attests. But this universal state of affairs assumes so many particular forms that they are often seen to be in conflict with one another. Contradiction? If so, we ought to find languages and money no less contradictory, because both are at once universal and particular. All cultures use language, all nations use money: the behavior is universal, but divided into languages, dialects, and accents, on the one hand, and into currencies, on the other; in each case there is rivalry and competition among them. And who would deny the universality of the sciences, themselves divided into a thousand specialties, not infrequently at odds with one another?

Conventions and virtualities—in a word, information: languages, mathematics, and monies, as well as holy texts and dogmas—all these things are incomparably useful in their application to the real world and to human societies. They are similar powers of a set of hot spots.

A Question for Our Time

We are experiencing today a global crisis that affects these four webs of relations all at once. Digital money, having become as invisible as the ancient king of Lydia, no longer stumbles or dawdles, but races around the planet in the blink of an eye. Digital processing, by ceaselessly generating and amplifying immense amounts of data, converts learning and knowledge into bits of information. We will no longer speak, we will no longer write as we did before; in the case of my own language, French, at least a fifth of its words have recently undergone change of one kind or another. Some religions are disappearing; others are moving backward and committing crimes; a few, inspired by compassion, continue to evolve. Deep transformations, all, that are changing the face, the appearance, and the potential uses of these four powers in ways that we are both exciting and disturbing.

Are we living once more in a crucial, axial age? Do we now find ourselves at the center of a hot spot? The answer, I strongly believe, is yes. The present moment harkens back to another, an ancient event that concerns all of the four innovations I have just described.

The Three Wise Men

Consider this presumptively mythical account. Caspar, Melchior, and Balthazar—possibly kings, surely scholars—rode across the desert for twelve days, guided by a star. According to an old tradition, each one represented a third of humanity; the entire inhabited world, in other words, the world in the process of becoming the one we live in today, was embarked on a journey.

As magi, and therefore sages, each excelled in a particular branch of knowledge. The first concerned himself with gold;

today we would call him an economist. Aromatic myrrh has medicinal properties, and so we would call the second one a botanist, perhaps a biochemist. And since frankincense had been used since the beginning of time to send praise, prayers, and entreaties to the gods, we would call the last one a poet. Wise men—thus the title that the foremost experts in their respective fields are awarded; today we would say that Caspar deserved to receive the Nobel Prize in economics, Melchior the prize in physics or medicine, and Balthazar the prize in literature or peace.

It was their learning, then, that made them powerful: the first understood the enormous force exerted by money in human affairs; the next, the promise of science and its medical applications; the last, the usefulness of language and communication. Together they understood the three powers capable of constructing or destroying things and groups of people, of making or unmaking kings, of bringing about endless war or perpetual peace. Did they invent these powers? We do not know; the most we can say is that their sumptuous gifts to the infant Jesus represented money, science, and language.

Incense and Language

From a censer emanate random twirls, fringed clouds of incense whose threads disperse in the air, visibly seeking to occupy space. After a time these scattered wisps vanish, as though they had just penetrated the imperceptible secret of extension, having passed through all the points of the space, like Peano's curve. Their fragrance, likewise invisible, spreads into the tiniest nooks and crannies. So too, carried along by the flight of its waves, the spoken word resonates and is heard here and there, more or less well, depending on the acoustics of the space and how acute the hearing of those who are listening; but it seeks to go everywhere. Wreaths of incense, granulations as fine and sensitive as alphabetical signs, mimic the diffusion of sound.

Let the spirit whisper and the soul spreads out in space, like a cloud of incense drifting haphazardly in search of ubiquity. For a long time I did not understand what prayer is, and I still have trouble. But it is enough to see incense wafting in the air. Incense and prayer both aspire to divine omnipresence.

Following a Star
The Three Kings, like true scholars, were forever searching. Traveling in the direction of a star, they dreamed of knowing the reasons for their wealth, for the royal authority that came from their *magical* learning, for the knowledge that came from their powers. For all serious scholars are curious to know more about the sources of their understanding and the secrets it may permit them to reveal; they are also motivated, it is true, by a desire for glory and a need for financing . . .

Where did the Wise Men come from? Perhaps from Persia, where a new religion had taken root. The name of its founder, Zoroaster, is thought to derive from the Avestan words for the camel and the stars—the means and the end of the journey of the Magi.

But whereas, following a point of reference very high in the sky, they were searching for a maximum, of power and glory, whose force could account for the explosive tensions that they held between their hands; and whereas they dreamed of reaching for the heavens, for the moon and the constellations, they found, after a long and exhausting transit, a newborn child laid down in a manger on a filthy bed of straw, surrounded by farm animals and an unregistered couple. Here, in other words, was a minimum, of wealth, learning, and language—a minimum they did not expect to find.

Searching for everything, they discovered nothing. They were searching for a king whose power was greater than their own three powers combined, in the immanence of the lands they passed through, under the firmament whose light shone down on them, and they discovered, inside a dimly lit grotto at night, three obscure homeless persons, surrounded by an ox and an ass, visited by local shepherds. They were seeking an energy that would transform the world, locally and globally; instead they discovered the subtle, almost empty strangeness of information.

They discovered, in other words, that the nothing of power and glory is everything. Money, science, and language—powerful, learned, of noble lineage—suddenly found themselves confronted, through religion, with the qualities of weakness, poverty, and humility. Strictly speaking, the Wise Men discovered religion *in its nascent state*.

On Epiphany

In ancient Greek, "epiphany" signified an appearance, a coming to light. This luminous manifestation arose from the short circuit of the two great revolutions I have just mentioned: one that gave birth to money, science, and the alphabet, symbolized by the Three Kings and their presents; the other from which emerged all the religions of Eurasia—in short, the short circuit among four universal networks, between our immanent powers and the extreme and transcendent weakness on which they depend.

Epiphany: the coming of the Magi to Bethlehem, the first manifestation of Christ. In suddenly interfering with the axial Eurasian emergence of benevolent and compassionate piety, the local, powerful, and aristocratic alliance of science, money, and language discovered the glowing hearth of the virtual, from which all true power and knowledge flow: *extreme fragility*. Did the infinite tenuousness of the virtual beget actual material power? Was the appearance of the pre-Socratic philosophers, initiators of the Greek miracle, the final episode of this axial age, the culmination of a series of events that swept over Eurasia like a tidal wave, a wave that at its crest brought with it the invention of geometry? If so, must we not see the Epiphany as completing and generalizing this "good news"?

To be sure, the Three Kings knew that their expertise derived from a virtual realm that was devoid of meaning and, for this reason, capable of being given any meaning at all; but as city dwellers, welcome in royal palaces (if these palaces were not in fact their own), they did not imagine that this virtual world could lie in the countryside, inside a cave, in the cradle of an infant child—in short, among the ordinary run of mortals, persons of no account, in a rural stable where a *newborn* slept in a manger, on a bed of straw.

This precious virtual world that is everywhere in our midst had its beginning there, saw the light of day there. It was hardly worth the trouble to travel so far and for so long, gazing upward, following a star, very high in the heavens—for the virtual lay right there, far below. You roam the whole world searching for truth, power, and fortune, and here they are, close at hand, beggars at your door. Here also, before the fire of an ordinary hearth, are gods. Hot spots can be found everywhere; everywhere and always the shining light of Epiphany is there to be seen.

Christmas in the Strict Sense

The luminosity of the Nativity reveals the meaning of the Gospel account, perhaps of my whole book. Appearance, emergence, birth, origin, source: money was born of its own absence, science came from ignorance, human speech began with the braying of an ass and the bellowing of a bull, religion appeared during the night, under the stars, among shepherds. Hot spots, all—they form the tectonic plate from which human cultures emerged. All these things, in their nascent state, are essentially religious in nature. It will therefore be necessary to understand where and how the energy that brought them forth was forged.

Power and Zerovalence

Kings bowed down before the powerless newborn child: money bowed down before homeless poverty; science bowed down before ignorance; language bowed down before silence—a silence broken by braying, bellowing, and babbling.

Did their intellect prevent the Magi from being deceived? Entranced, enraptured, they reckoned the distance between the star and the child, between the necessary sovereignty of a light that illuminated the whole world, everywhere, and the fragile contingency of a life just beginning, here, in Bethlehem. Thus ubiquity came suddenly to be concentrated in a small point. From infinite pressure, infinite density, came enormous energy.

Wise men, if not also kings, each one powerful by virtue of his particular expertise, they came to realize that their importance, their finitude floated in this open range, between star and child, between kings and shepherds, between nothing and everything; that not only their gifts, symbolic of their persons and their professions, but the world itself lies somewhere in the range between minimal weakness and maximal strength, between the nilpotent and omnipotence, between omnivalence and zerovalence, between *almighty energy* and *frail information*. They came to realize that God, if he exists, sleeps in the silent depths of fragility as much as he illuminates space and time. Here is the gap religions require, the energy from which they issue and the energy they propagate. This hot spot is known as Incarnation.

The Three Kings of power, the Wise Men of science carried with them all values; they traveled so great a distance because they hoped to reach the highest value of all, the star, at the roof of the heavens; in the end they arrived at the null value, straw. The Epiphany therefore unveiled our destiny, wobbling in this open range between everything and nothing, between being and nothingness, as the learned would say; in sum, this indefinite totality, this capacity, this virtuality that no doubt defines what is human—or rather, what is divine. Divine and human, they are called Incarnation.

Not only emergence, but also explosion. A big bang.

A Provisional Balance Sheet

The light of the Epiphany came down from the short circuit between the two thunderbolts that changed the history of the world then thought to be inhabited. Has there ever been a more crucial moment in human history? Has there ever been a hotter spot than this, so burning and luminous it is called Epiphany?

That night in Bethlehem, improbably enough, three kings in majesty bowed down before a pitiable newborn child. From this *mythical but honest falsehood* emanated the epiphanic light of a moment that can be dated with precision: 6 January, according to our calendar. Later I will talk in greater detail about the distinction between the dishonestly true and the honestly false. For the time being it is enough to say that forgeries in painting, like false news, seem to be genuine, whereas almost all the dogmas of religion (or at least the ones with which I am familiar), though they are not true, do not seek to deceive: virginity after giving birth, resurrection, Epiphany, and so on. This last myth, as we have just seen, conceals a profound historical reality.

Rereading Historiography

Midas, Gyges, and Croesus invented money in Phrygia and Lydia; Thales and Pythagoras invented rigorous science; the names of those who compressed letters into an alphabet are unknown to us; the names of those who in Eurasia founded the religions of the axial age I mentioned earlier. And then there are Caspar, Melchior, and Balthazar themselves. Modern historians, employing perfectly sound methods, have found no documentary evidence for their existence, at least not in the case of the Magi or the kings of Greek myth, which remains fabricated, imaginary, symbolic. And yet the more common this hypercritical approach to historiography has become in our time, the more surprising it seems that money, science, writing, and the major religions, all of them due to legendary or quasi-legendary figures, should have lasted longer in time and spread further in space than the empires founded by actual persons, such as Genghis Khan, Alexander, Caesar, and Napoleon, whose historical existence and mortal exploits are well attested.

How is it that spiritual power, light, impalpable, ethereal, tends toward ubiquity and permanence, whereas temporal power, heavy and local, is subject to decreasing returns in space and time? The pharaohs reigned longer than the emperors of Rome, whose domination was more enduring than that of the British Empire, whose mastery of the world lasted longer than that of the United States. Why should soft power last longer and bind more securely than hard power? The more complete the triumph of hypercritical historiography, the better it shows, however unwillingly, the extent to which the imaginary figures of legendary texts enjoy a strange universality. It is altogether as though information, rare and fragile, is more resistant over the long term than energy, fatally linked to the growth of entropy.

Lateral lesson: myths, stories, old wives' tales, balderdash, the Three Kings of biblical tradition, the carved figures of a Provençal Christmas crib or a figurine hidden in a king cake on Epiphany—why should these incredibly tenuous things matter more, in respect of actual historical experience, than many more things that have been solidly documented? Why should they influence what are taken to be facts, objective, deep-seated in historical memory, and decisive, just as the tectonic plates revealed by volcanic eruptions have sculpted the continents and influenced events on the surface of the earth? I therefore now see the Epiphany as the moment when all these inventions were bound together, in a knot, in a sort of ligature. Thus, in keeping with its doubtful etymology, religion binds together.

Theoretical Interlude
Henri Bergson, writing about the two sources of morality and religion, manifestly had Carnot's theorem in mind.

Thermodynamics, the science of energy, was a constant source of inspiration to him, even with regard to the titles he gave his books. He was working at a time when the great rivalry in the natural sciences was between the upholders of Boltzmann's theory of entropy and Darwin's theory of evolution. Time is surely irreversible. But is it increasing or decreasing?

In developing his arguments concerning temporal duration, Bergson, like Comte before him, went no further than statics and dynamics. Thermodynamics, a new field, from which he drew his distinction between the open and the closed, represented an advance over the classical mechanics of the positivists. Bergson therefore hesitated between two bodies of knowledge and the methods that could be derived from each of them. My dream, in relation to religion, is to speak of two sources as well: *energy flanked by entropy* and *information*, both born of the same science of fire.

The distinction between the open and the closed, whose importance was rightly insisted upon by Bergson himself and which was famous already in his time, is not as simple as Bergson claimed. For a closed system is eventually exhausted by entropy, in the dark, the cold, and the encroaching emptiness; but an open system, unprotected, exposed to winds, frosts, microbes, disappears still more rapidly. Indeed, everything that exists is closed and open at the same time: an atom adorns itself with one or several valences; a membrane envelops a molecule, but small holes perforate its surface; bars, screens, and shutters close the openings, the doors and windows of a house; organs, connected to the totality of a body, perform their specialized functions; a locked greenhouse lets in the sun . . . Why should animal and human societies be exceptions to this universal rule? Every system dies from entropy and survives from information, whose power is minute, by contrast, and which is dense in its rarity.

Where Does the Energy of Religion Come From?

This energy comes from three short circuits.

Religion concentrates the world, filled with nymphs and suffused with divine glory, in a society, a family, even the depths of one's being. It binds an immense exterior with a tiny interior. The world is in me and in us, I am, we are the world.

Religion also concentrates the whole, permeated with God's omnipresence, in the place carved out by the group and the quasi-null point that I occupy. The whole is I, this nothing that is everything.

Finally, religion begins from nothing and invades the existing; virtual, imaginary, mythical, invisible; though it is spiritual, it moves the actual, crowds and individual persons alike.

These three short circuits—the immense concentrated in the point, everything in nothing, being in nothingness—produce pressures at infinite energy densities whose release sometimes causes the explosion, throughout the course of time, of destructive hatred and the love that creates civilizations.

Big bang!

Myth, History

Let us return now to myths, which should be taken seriously, precisely because they appeared before rational knowledge was born. In this connection I like to give the example of terrestrial paradise as it is described in Genesis. Neither historians nor you nor I give any credence to this story of apple and rib. Myth, fable, call it what you will, nothing in any case. And yet for some time now prehistorians have been telling us how happy the life of our hunter-gatherer ancestors must have been (Adam and Eve seem only to have gathered), exempt as they were from the merciless wars between agriculturalists and pastoralists that began in the Neolithic: Cain killed Abel. With the cultivation of the soil and the raising of crops, a brilliant invention, it became necessary to close off the fields from all animal incursion, in order to protect fragile seeds, flowering cereals, and ripening vegetables against the ravages of cows, pigs, and flocks driven by herdsmen.

The generation separating Eve from Abel spans two eras that are well known to archeologists specializing in prehistory, during the course of which the right to property seems first to have appeared, ushering in an abominable chapter of human history rife with murder and conflict. What would you do if a troop of oxen trampled your seed corn and then devoured it? The first person who thought of closing off his field, saying, in effect, this is mine—to me, that person was the inventor of warlike violence; he killed the first person who overstepped a boundary. The death of Remus repeated and completed that of Abel.

Myths therefore announce dense, powerful truths, expressed differently than the truths of accounts duly corroborated by those honest persons whom we venerate as historians; meticulous in establishing the authenticity of our record of the facts, they therefore despise such fables, which nonetheless, which sometimes . . .

Return to the Present
Once more I retrace my steps. Let us recall the Feast of the Epiphany and the four networks—money, science, language, and religion—now in crisis and undergoing transformation.

Political life today has broken down because we no longer have a philosophy of history. Until not long ago, politics was founded on the philosophy inaugurated by the Enlightenment, a secular translation of the term "Epiphany," a Voltairean way of rereading Saint John the Apostle. Adam Smith, theoretician of liberalism, and Karl Marx, prophet of socialism, lived, acted, and thought as the philosophers of the Enlightenment did. We are now witnessing the extinction of these two opposed tendencies, which grew out of a common trunk; more generally, we are witnessing a crisis of reason, described in the first instance by these same Enlightenment thinkers.

The collapse that is currently underway began with the flash of lightning at Hiroshima, and then at Nagasaki, where a science reputed to be wholly and uniquely good committed crimes against humanity, massacred innocents, in a tragically incendiary spot. Today we are the survivors of this crisis and of this burning, where the energy expended was proportionate to the crime.

Before the rise and fall of the Enlightenment, there shone the light of myths and religions, the light that John the Evangelist, mistrusting experience, said shines in the darkness, the light that darkness has not overcome. This light is Epiphany—so powerful that it brings together, as we have just seen, in a blinding short circuit, all of our thoughts, activities, behaviors, ideals. Here we gain access to the tectonic plates of history.

The Massacre of the Innocents
It is written in Matthew (2:1–16) that the three royal visitors came to inform Herod, who was then king in Jerusalem, of the new birth, and that Herod then decreed that all newborn

male children be put to death. How could it be said any more clearly than this that even inventions as marvelous as science, language, money, and religion can be deadly once they come near to power?

With regard once again to the Epiphany: for a light to illuminate, there must be an emission source. No clarity without fire, which shines and burns at the same time. The reason of the Enlightenment, wholly optimistic, only saw light shine. But on the day of Hiroshima and for years afterward, the light of reason grew dark from burning, from incinerating thousands of innocent people. The light of the Epiphany, more prudent, more realistic, announced not only the advent of the Christian religion, but also the massacres of innocents yet to come. Beforehand, joy at the birth of a divine child; later, the terrors unleashed by the Apocalypse. An explosively hot spot, a place of fire, in the vicinity of power.

The association of wise men and kings, of learning and power, of force and religions, risks tipping over at any moment into horror. The Three Wise Men disappeared from the Gospel account as suddenly as they had come, leaving behind the prospect of unspeakable slaughter, the obscene butchering of so many newborns. The savage conflagration at this hot spot blazed with an intense light. Another open range of our capacities, between the joy of Jesus's birth and revulsion at the prospect of unending murder, between heaven and hell. Earlier I mentioned the Persian religion, which taught the existence of two opposed gods, Good and Evil. As a descendant of the Cathar tradition, which flourished in southern France toward the end of the Middle Ages, I understand this duality, prior traces of which are found in the tale of Zoroaster's magi and in Empedocles's law of Love and Strife.

History teaches all of this with an overabundance of examples. Mastery of language and of the communication it makes possible, occupying space like incense, led to the spread of ideologies that, as I well remember and always fear, kill in great numbers. Language, as we have known since Aesop, is the best and the worst of things; likewise, as we have known since Aristotle (and later Freud), money, diabolical in its power to persuade people that anyone desiring to have as much of it as they do must be done away with. The ferocious contests of language and money are destroying the planet. A small number of people today, abominable gods of our modern Olympus, have as much personal wealth as the poorest half of humanity. Since the Enlightenment, whose illumination was extinguished at Hiroshima, since the invention of bow and cannon, and the more refined arts of bombardment that came from that, we have known that science, the best and worst of things, can inspire us to work toward peace or to build arms of mass destruction.

The masteries of wise men and kings have therefore often caused the death of innocents. The Epiphany emitted a decisive light, whose dual meaning, peaceable and criminal, illuminates our decisions and our deeds, our fortunes and misfortunes, the course of our lives and our freedom of choice. A hot spot, to be sure, but one that both shines and burns, shines with rare sanctity and burns with unholy energy.

We should mistrust the powers of the learned.

Hot Spot at Hiroshima

Threatened, temporary, joyously incarnate, my life flowed from Hiroshima. On that day of wrath, Japanese women, children, and older people were transformed by the thousands into human torches by a pilot bearing a gift come from on high named "Little Boy," the atomic bomb, it too in a nascent state. Noel, a newborn come down from the sky! What an Epiphany—what a massacre of innocents!

No doubt the pilot of the murderous airplane played only the role of an angelic intermediary in this tragedy; perhaps also the American president, Harry S. Truman, who with horrendous cruelty ordered the two bombings. But what are we to say of the famous physicists who, pondering and calculating in the peace and calm of the New Mexico desert, in the purest abstraction, made the first weapon of mass destruction capable of killing so many human beings? Are we to say that, however learned they may have been, they were unaware, they did not know what they were doing? What then are we to say of their successors, aware since Nagasaki, who worked ceaselessly to amplify this destructive force in order to create a thermonuclear weapon, the hydrogen bomb? Mathematical physics and its Enlightenment came down to earth once more, only this time to bring death by fire to thousands of innocents.

On that day I thought I saw again the sun of Joshua, the sun that had been argued over in the trial of Galileo; a few specialists in murder on a large scale had ratified the verdict, in effect, in order to hurl the fire of this sun down upon their fraternal enemies. Although my body lived far from this hot spot, my burned soul, my turned head were born that morning. I was born in this epiphanic light.

The period of my childhood and youth, steeped in criminal ideologies, continues to show us how great the cost in human lives the sun's descent to earth may be, turning a wondrous equation into a deadly weapon, from the newborn Christ to the massacre of the innocents, from theoretical abstraction to political practice, socialist and Nazi alike; in short, it speaks to us still of spiritual power in the temporal realm. Nothing is more difficult to control than the hot spot of Incarnation—a halo that may spread salvific grace or explode in every direction.

Secular Equivalent of the Epiphany

The festival of the Epiphany, popular in countries where Romance languages are spoken, therefore evokes a temporal intersection, the knot that links the three epochal Ionian discoveries—money, science, written language—and the axial age that during the course of the same century suddenly came into being throughout Eurasia. In the wake of the immense tidal wave that eventually swept over Greece in the West, philosophy emerged there, pre-Socratic to begin with, then enriched by the thought of Plato, Aristotle, Epicurus, Plotinus, and others.

At this crucial moment it is difficult to separate the inventions of physics and geometry, to which I called attention earlier, describing them as hot spots, from the appearance of philosophy, no less burning in its way. The pre-Socratics included physicists, and Thales, as we have seen, is said to have invented the first mathematical theorem, which bears his name still today. The whole Greek miracle, science and philosophy taken together, therefore marks the temporal intersection between the three Ionian discoveries and the Western extremity of the axial age. The Greek miracle—an abstraction without a god—may be seen as another Epiphany. Renan did not have to travel any very great distance, leaving Noel behind in Palestine, in order to call this prior Noel, on the Acropolis, a miracle. Why should we not call it "good news" as well?

Lightning and hot spot: illuminated by the sun, outside the cave, Platonic Ideas came down to earth. They carried within them the whole of the virtual world, the abstract in its entirety; they promised therefore the sciences in their entirety. And, since ideas are daughters of idols, idols become root stocks. Plato very well described the sudden insight that led from the Idea of a table to a particular table. Were all such realizations hot spots? With Galileo, mathematical physics was later to give a precise meaning to this journey from the ideal to the real.

All of this has to do with what I call the cognitive. *Objective* knowledge began with a short circuit between another world and our world. But a hot spot can also bring into existence not only the *subjective*, which is to say the individual, but also the *collective*, which is to say a community of individuals.

The Transfigured Individual

And after six days Jesus took with him Peter and James and John his brother, and led them up a high mountain apart. And he was transfigured before them, and his face shone like the sun, and his garments became as white as light. And behold, there appeared to them Moses and Elijah, talking with him. And Peter said to Jesus, "Lord, it is well that we are here; if you wish, I will make three tabernacles here, one for you and one for Moses and one for Elijah." He was still speaking, when lo, a bright cloud overshadowed them, and a voice from the cloud said, "This is my beloved Son, with whom I am well pleased; listen to him." When the disciples heard this, they fell on their faces, and were filled with awe. But Jesus came

and touched them, saying, "Rise, and have no fear." And
when they lifted up their eyes, they saw no one but Jesus
only. And as they were coming down the mountain, Jesus
commanded them, "Tell no one the vision, until the Son
of Man is raised from the dead."

And the disciples asked him, "Then why do the scribes
say that first Elijah must come?" He replied, "Elijah is
indeed coming first, and he is to restore all things; but
I tell you that Elijah has already come, and they did not
know him, but did to him whatever they pleased. So
also the Son of Man will suffer at their hands." Then the
disciples understood that he was speaking to them of
John the Baptist.

Matthew 17:1–9

The sun no longer shines in the tetrahedron and the pyramid, no longer burns in the *gnomon*; now it illuminates a
person. The cognitive light no longer emanates from the
objective but bursts into the subjective. The brilliance of the
Epiphany is transported, permanently, to the summit of a
mountain. Later, the Passion was to massacre this innocent.
I see Jesus reborn, transfigured by intuition, unrecognizable, as upright and knowing as the shaft of a sundial; and
the apostles, thrown to the ground, prostrate around this
well of light.

Hot Spot of the Ego

"There is neither Jew nor Greek, neither slave nor free, neither male nor female . . ." Thus Saint Paul (Galatians 3:28)
delivered human beings from their various corporate attachments, which imprison them, tie them down; he unbound

them, personalized them. Now, then, through Jesus Christ, I am in direct contact with God. *Ego credo*: it is I who believe; or rather, this faith creates the self.

From her inert mass of marble, Saint Teresa rises up in ecstasy. She receives the fire, like a blade, in the body. She exists, because ecstasy and existence derive from the same Greek root; they say something analogous. The saint becomes a hot spot surrounded by a nimbus, a brilliant halo. I am enraptured, therefore I am.

Art and the Other World

The volcanic burning of the hot spot explodes in the middle of the forehead and forearm of Jeremiah, in Rembrandt's *Jeremiah Lamenting the Destruction of Jerusalem* (1630), and on the wall behind Christ, shown in profile in his first version of the *Supper at Emmaus* (1629). In both pictures Rembrandt depicts the flashing short circuit produced by the other world descending like a bolt of lightning on this one. In both pictures the figures seem to vanish in the presence of such a light, whose brilliance transfigures and effaces them.

In Raphael's painting *The Transfiguration* (ca. 1520), in the lower part of the canvas, we see men who are blind to what is happening, except for a boy whose dead eyes look toward and very clearly see what no one else sees, the scene in the upper part of the canvas, which represents what transcends representation. So far from representing the visible, what is called classical painting, or at least its masterpieces, make the invisible visible—that which we cannot recognize, do not even know how to recognize. Might I call this picture by Raphael a metacanvas, in the sense that it is the womb of all such masterpieces, the root stock, the source from which the attempt to render the invisible visible sprang?

The other world descends on Jeremiah and the pilgrims to Emmaus as it is revealed and speaks in Fra Angelico's chaste and mute *Annunciation* (ca. 1440–45). Was not the popular success of Millet's *Angelus* (1857–59) due to the fact that the picture allows us to see and hear the world that descends, invisibly, upon the two praying peasants?

Brilliantly represented, the figures of these paintings display what has no form, what cannot be displayed. Let a work of art be connected to a hot spot and the centuries have no hold over it. They are as everlasting as Thales's theorem and the Feast of the Epiphany.

Air and Fire

Can this same fire also descend upon a community of individuals? Combine its parts into one thing? Something long-lasting? Something like humanity?

> When the day of Pentecost had come, [the apostles] were all together in one place. And suddenly a sound came from heaven like the rush of a mighty wind, and it filled all the house where they were sitting. And there appeared to them tongues as of fire, distributed and resting on each one of them. And they were all filled with the Holy Spirit and began to speak in other tongues, as the Spirit gave them utterance.
>
> Acts of the Apostles 2:1–4

In keeping with the Jewish tradition of the Revelation on Mount Sinai, which this episode renewed by enlarging its scope of application, the image of fire materializes the divine

Voice. From this place there radiated the languages of the world: the apostles began to speak "in tongues," and everyone understood them; or rather, all groups, all societies were born of this federation, which is inspired by a fierce ideology toward others, tolerant and altruistic. Pentecost inverts the Passion: whereas in that case everyone is reconciled by killing the victim, here the same victim, having once again become divine, unites everyone.

Now, no one has heard an orator as multiple as the apostles of Pentecost; their speech is called a miracle. No, it was not a miracle. Let such an orator now turn around, take a piece of chalk, and write on the blackboard a system of differential equations to which he has just found solutions; behind him, in an amphitheater, a thousand mathematicians from around the world, all speaking different languages, take notes, then leap to their feet, acclaiming his discovery. Now let him take a baton and turn to face an international orchestra; he distributes scores and each performer, no matter what language he or she speaks, takes part in the symphony, each playing their own instrument. The audience rises to its feet, cheering. In both cases, everyone has understood, the miracle has taken place.

Long may they live, music and mathematics, both endowed with universality. New holy scriptures?

Deus Absconditus

Can we build a puteal, a wall around the hot spot of which I speak? Ask yourself this. Has God removed himself to his Kingdom, hidden from our world? Or rather: has divine ubiquity disappeared in the quasi-empty volume of an expanding universe, which at every one of its points shows this omnipresence under the aspect of an immense nonpresence? Does the most miniscule of miniscule particles conceal God's vacancy, veil his transcendent absence? Present everywhere, infinitely, he is nowhere apparent. Transfinite and continuous, like a point on the real number line, unique and indivisible. Point and sign, as Euclid put it, at the very beginning of the *Elements*.

And yet Christians claim still, more than two thousand years later, that God became incarnate. A gigantic contraction reduced, compressed, crammed his universal absence into a place of supernatural density where his immanent body and blood lay, present and finite. The first God is absent, the second is present. The one is virtual, diluted to the point of pure emptiness, utterly missing, nowhere to be found in this world; the other is real, exceedingly dense, concentrated to an incomparable degree, present here, in this very place.

Archaic, simple, and incomprehensible, the filial and paternal relation between the two can now be seen to be a powerful connection, subtle and rational, a duality that obtains between universal and singular, global and local; between an infinite immensity and a finite pinpoint here; between the virtual and the real, the absent and the present. The other world, in its globality, strikes somewhere, one spot in particular, suddenly, in dense and concentrated form. Here, and once more, the hot spot is called Incarnation.

Being

During the Reformation, Catholics and Protestants clashed over the question of the so-called Real Presence: were the bread and wine consecrated by the sacrament of the Eucharist *really* the body and blood of Christ, or were these foods to be understood only in a symbolic sense, as mere signs?

The implications of this quarrel, whose fine points hold little interest for most people today, were nonetheless profound. By calling into question the very meaning of the verb "to be," so commonly used, both because and in spite of the fact that it is null and universal at the same time, omnipotent and zerovalent, it was to have lasting consequences, notably for the attitude of whole nations toward commerce and its monetary instruments: did money have a real value or was it nothing more than a symbolic representation of value? Should we prefer gold to paper money, the thing to the convention, the real presence to the empty sign—in short, this world of ours to the other, virtual world? Paradoxically, since it favored the symbol, the wealth of nations soon came to depend on this choice.

Temple

But cultural attitudes also had decisive consequences for the built environment. Here I am thinking in particular of religious structures, those buildings where no one lives and where crowds gather. How are we to define and design a temple, for example? The word itself derives from the Greek *temnein*, meaning "to cut" (note, by the way, that *atomos*, the source of our word "atom," signifies that which cannot be cut, cannot be divided into parts). A temple cuts up a profane space and marks out one or more sacred places within it. Another kind of puteal, then.

Consider the way in which the Temple of Solomon in Jerusalem partitioned space: first the Outer Court, where the people assembled to worship; after that the Inner Court (or Court of the Priests); then the Holy Place; finally, the Holy of Holies, reserved solely for the use of the High Priest and containing the Ark of the Covenant, guarded by two cherubim. Here we proceed from one sanctuary to another, each one denser in holiness than the last. And how are we to think of a synagogue? As a place of assembly—the meaning of its very name, again from the Greek, *synagōgē*.

Both before and after the Reformation, by contrast, a cathedral was not primarily a place of assembly, where worshippers gathered together more or less briefly, or, for longer periods of time, a chapter of canons, nor a sacred place marked off from a profane space; it was a structure inhabited, permanently and in fact, by a body and its blood, both actually present. Whether Gothic or Romanesque, a cathedral *was* and *is* a place where Christ himself lives, where he is carnally present.

We come, then, to a question that is at once theological and architectural: how can one build a house where the living, actually present God resides, that is, a place in which divine ubiquity, forever and everywhere distributed in the universe, is concentrated, humble, small, infinitely concentrated, almost atomic—the global God in the body of the infinitesimal Incarnate?

Reason, Energy

The Western philosophical tradition has not ceased to admire the austere proportions of Greek temples, with their triangular pediments and parallel columns, which embody in space the serenity of geometry and the harmony of reason. Who lives there, in these temples? *Logos*, of course; the Greek word means word or speech. But above all, though only among the Greeks and their successors, reason and proportion, *ratio vel proportio*. In a word, *information*.

Why did the curve of the Roman vault and the intrados of the Gothic arch suddenly replace the perpendicular and

oblique lines from which geometry had descended long before? On account of the process of concentration I have
already described. The miniscule place occupied by this real
presence collects and gathers up, almost atomically, in the
root sense of the word—for a Christian church is not a Hebrew temple—the whole vast universe of divine absence. The
idea of a God living here, in this very place, means that an
ubiquitous presence, distributed throughout all of creation,
is concentrated in an infinitesimal black box, in which there
reigns a supernatural density whose pressure integrates, ac-
cumulates so much *energy* that it shines, that it burns, that it
is always on the verge of exploding and once again spreading throughout the universe. A big bang—I told you! The
sun, once again: now it's inside the cathedral! Quick, try to
control this deflagration, keep it from spreading, contain
it with massive quantities of rocks! Bomb alert! An atomic
bomb has gone off inside the cathedral!

If the Greek temple was composed of calm rectangles,
in keeping with the dictates of reason, serene, accessible,
and finite, though secretly haunted by disturbing irrational diagonals, the Christian cathedral was forced to bend
under the volcanic pressure of this sudden blast. Whereas
the Greek temple is a monument to cold reason, the Christian cathedral is a hot spot, explosive, burning, burned.
From the Middle Ages onward its volume grew, increased
and swelled, under the effect of a deflagration whose terrifying power emanated from the tabernacle—originally,
in ancient Israel, a tent—at the upper center of the altar.
Thus the pointed arches of the Gothic, the gleaming rays of
the monstrance, and the resplendent colors of the stained-
glass windows propagated, in every direction, from a tiny
pinpoint, the shock waves of the bomb's blast, real and

immanent, radiating through the totality of the empty space; the surrounding structure became curved, here in the shape of a circle, there of an ogive, there again, in the nave, of the hull of an overturned boat, under the force of this terrific upheaval; everywhere buttresses and flying buttresses, helping to stave off the threat of collapse, permanent and virtual, from the explosion. Quick, bolster the walls of country churches with thick stones, also the naves of collegiate churches, so that their massive weight will trap, conserve, control the force of the blast—as though this weight was meant to offset the awesome power of grace.

Refracting the glowing blue of the forge, the flashing red of the furnace, the incandescent and polychrome brilliance of the volcano, the stained glass shot through by the nuclear light issuing from this fulmination is dazzling. It is as though, inside, a caldera has been set ablaze by an eruption, sending forth scarlet streams of lava glowing through the rose window.

We call the tiny dwelling place of the Eucharist a tabernacle, which is to say a tent, for we know that at the beginning of our era you, a Jew, were wandering in Galilee, miserable, without a home, like your ancestors, who journeyed through the desert, searching, as you yourself were, for the Promised Land and the Kingdom beyond this world. Do not leave the stone nave we have just constructed for you. Settle down at last, do not abandon us, do not resume your nomadic wandering in this enormous, diluted world, from which your omnipresent Father has removed himself. I beg you, stay with us, for night is falling; sup with us, we who are truly present, spread yourself through the universe in an immense absence, like that of God, though he is everywhere present. In this tabernacle, beneath these massings of stone, round and ogival, we shelter your fearsome virtual power.

Another Puteal, Another Tabernacle

Draw the two descending branches of any angle you like from a single point. At some distance from the apex, form a triangle by drawing a straight line between the two branches. Now let this new side slide up and down. It becomes shorter the closer it comes to the apex.

Now drop a line bisecting this angle and let it pass through all the degrees of the angle; these lines, taken together, cut up the third side into segments of various lengths. It is as though this lateral range makes it possible to align, even to count, the points of the third side, which moves as well. From this it follows that there exist as many points on the long sides as on the short sides. Taken to an unimaginable limit, this means that there are as many points at the apex as on the third side, however long it may be.

We saw earlier that Euclid, at the beginning of the *Elements*, said that a point has no parts. Cantor, by contrast, at the end of the nineteenth century, was to say that a point contains parts having a continuous transfinite power. The infinite, he announced, is a set whose parts have the same power as the whole.

Here we have two ways of coming back to the puteal. The one, mathematical: the transfinite is concentrated in an accumulation point that is beyond our comprehension. The other, ecclesiastical: the ubiquity contracts, becomes incarnate, concentrated in a place of supernatural density: world, cathedral, tabernacle, host. The opposite progression, from the miniscule to the universal, I take to be a terrifying explosion, an incredibly big bang—big enough to bend the stones themselves, shatter the stained glass into molten splinters, melt the rose windows in flames.

Cathedral Under Stress
The spasmodic violence has not yet exhausted itself. One of the largest cities in the world sprawls beneath Popocatépetl, the awakened volcano whose smoking dome overlooks it, from the height of its snows, without being seen by the city, blind, drowned in the fog of its own pollution; wracked by fierce upheavals, the city goes on sinking, without hope, into the old lake of Tenochtitlán, poorly filled in; the city's buildings slowly subside. A hot spot draws it toward the abyss. The Palace of Fine Arts, built of marble, sinks three centimeters a year; to enter, visitors descend into a crypt by stairways that their parents once climbed. The whole center of the city is moving, the walls of the streets induce vertigo and seasickness. A place where nature preempts any attempt to counteract its effects; fire, air, and water threaten the earth of Mexico City.

Nearby, built partly of stones salvaged from the temple that reigned in splendor at the center of the ancient Aztec capital, the immense Metropolitan Cathedral, with its two towers and two facades, a masterpiece of Christian architecture, is also in a state of advancing decay. Overrun by a forest of metal scaffolding, traversed from the top of its vault to the floor by a steel cable whose enormous plumb seems disorientingly to diverge from the vertical; here the floor totters to the left, there falls off to the right, elsewhere lurches forward; retables tilt, statues lean sideways; crevasses and branching cracks suggest the cathedral is likely to break up before it sinks from sight. Civil engineers have valiantly tried to save it from this last fate by injecting concrete into the foundations, but shocks from the subway line below—another form of thunder, this time subterranean—only undermine them further. Pitching, rolling, listing, this cathedral, more than her sisters, deserves to be likened to a ship on the sea—a ship in distress: the horizontal bent beneath the weight of shifting masses of stone, the walls split by the shuddering floor, the paintings and sculpted gilding hidden by a thousand metal stays and struts and tie beams in imminent danger of being torn apart; for the moment, at least, they still hold together. Symbol and summary of the city, the great cathedral writhes in pain. Will it manage to cheat its chthonic destiny? No, it will die. When? To what lull in what millennial hurricane do I owe the privilege of visiting the parts of the cathedral that are still open to the public, the ones that are thought to pose less of a threat to life and limb than the others? The mighty carcass struggles against its inevitable end.

Deprived of equilibrium, the cathedral nonetheless lives on. It succumbs slowly. Until now, it has resisted exploding.

In this same place, the Zócalo, the main plaza of Mexico City, three structures face one other, forming a rectangle. At the corner separating the cathedral from the presidential palace, looking out upon a public market, a riot of colors, voices, and fragrances, there once stood a pyramid, now in ruins, whose steps, scarcely four hundred years ago, measured out the moments of time in anticipation of the future coming of Quetzalcoatl, the feathered serpent with the face of an old man. Did the Aztecs therefore realize, before we did, that birds came from reptiles and that our species, *Homo sapiens*, completed this evolution? Did they fittingly place this discovery at the summit of a temporal scale? Do we understand what this towering clock symbolized, this line of evolutionary descent, this *gnomon*, knowing time-counter of the living world? Did the civilizations that came before us and that we eradicated begin by knowing life, whereas we have ended up being ignorant of it, whereas we do not cease to destroy it? This representation in stone of the vertical eruption of the everlasting, a device for following the path of the sun and the god's earthly progress—this temple, today, lies in ruins, overgrown by historical death and oblivion. But did not the Aztec priests also feed the god with the blood and flesh of their horrible sacrifices, massacres of innocents? The point of contact between the invisible and the visible remained on high, in the bodies of those who died by torture—another figure of the one who was crucified atop Golgotha.

On one side of this temple, then, conquered by a foreigner who may have known less about its chronometric purpose than did the temple itself, stands the presidential palace, which behind a long and monotonous façade is decorated with gaudy frescos relating the triumph of politics, with Marx pictured as its apotheosis, an almighty bearded God in majesty, looking down upon the masses—a piece of mime, soon to be obsolete, after the model of the Sistine Chapel. On the other side of the temple, the cathedral sinks from the action of telluric forces. Opening onto the rest of the rectangle are shops and restaurants; from their terraces one is given to admire one of the most beautiful public spaces in the world, swarming with life under the influence of three kinds of death: the human sacrifices of the Aztecs at the summit of their pyramidal shrines, political forgetfulness, and the subsidence of buildings amidst the upheavals of war and earth.

Which of these deaths should we fear most? Should we dread above all the power of the presidency, whose past incumbents are vividly memorialized by the richly colored portraits hanging in the halls of the palace; its corrupt police, who kill openly, in the streets, and with impunity; the malign influence of money and arms, crueler than the violence of the volcano not far to the north, which sustains the poverty of this rich country and conspires, through the executions carried out by drug lords and their allies, to prevent its people from ruling themselves, free from terror? Should we tremble instead before the summit of the pyramid, where the priest cloaked himself in the skin of a victim he had just flayed alive? Or should we shudder on entering the cathedral, anxiously reckoning the hour of its collapse? Marx has already joined Moctezuma and Cortés underground, where the cathedral accompanies the pyramid and the palace in their gradual decline, powers in unstable equilibrium on the viscosity of the lake. Time kills death and death kills time.

Now too old to fear men and names, I prefer fire, air, water, and earth; volcano, breeze, lake, seismic activity. Mexico delivers its people from politics; at the summit of power, the public spaces empty, little by little. The buttresses of the cathedral will not long protect it from sinking: I know, because I imitate it, its hopeless battle; like the cathedral, I inhabit this labile remainder of time, planted like the spine of a binding in the centuries of centuries; I reside in the same fragile angle, suspended like a pendulum; fearing the same interval, I fight in vain against subsidence, against suffocation beneath the compact loam; leaning, my walls crack, my vault cleaves; I haunt this masonry and share in the vertigo of its mortal struggle; my feet are balanced on its slanting horizontal ribs, my skeleton stands upright, pressed up against its sloping vertical ribs; my own ribs tremble with its crevices, my bones are linked together like its iron bar chains, my muscles tighten like its taut buttresses, my head is caught in its ruined dome; our twin vessels sing joyfully the song of this long unsteadiness—O my body of Samson, whose force shook the columns of the temple! What secret makes us, the cathedral and me, explode with life, blaze with power and joy? My emotion, true motion, bursts forth vertically from our joint descent. The eternal victory of death recoils before the insolent defiance of weakness, during the brief moment of passion that is mine.

May religion triumph and forget religion. In the process of crumbling, of dying, it survives by not being able to survive down here, for it is purified and becomes religion only by forsaking law and politics, temporal power, financial wealth. The Church shall surely triumph when the new Jerusalem comes down from heaven, but for the moment it soldiers on, here and now, as I do, welcoming with open arms the earth that conquers us in each fresh combat.

On Good Friday the earth quaked. No doubt the wood of the Cross lost the verticality of its axis and the horizontal line of its arms. Constructed on the geometry of this tree, the cathedral shakes. My trunk bound to its leaning axis, my arms hanging from its sloping transversal, my prostrate body shares in the fate of the one who was crucified. The people of the Third World, poor, weighed down by sorrows, but better off than multitudes of the rich and the powerful—only they understand Christianity, life in a state of disequilibrium, in short, the Incarnation, here realized in one of the hottest spots in the world, which burns from the encounter between the shaking ground and a trembling humanity, but also from the encounter between the Real Presence and the weight of stones massed to protect it.

Telluric upheavals, historic events, religious tabernacles, flying buttresses—so many things punctuating very different times.*

Durations Compared

Whether or not one accepts the hypothesis of an axial age, the fact remains, I repeat, that Confucianism, Buddhism, and Judaism have endured for three thousand years, are still active and revered, against all odds; Christianity for two thousand years, Islam for fifteen hundred. Geometry has endured for two thousand five hundred years; physics, for five hundred . . . During these long intervals, how many empires were born, flourished, and declined before finally collapsing? Egyptian pharaohs, petty Greek kings and their city-states, the Roman Empire, feudalism, Genghis Khan and Attila, the German Holy Roman Empire, the Norman invasion, Spanish conquests, Italian provinces, Charles V, the Sun King, Napoleon, the British Empire, the United States, China—I enumerate at random this chaos of tinkerings with the course of history. During the time when these frail existences were born and successively disappeared, first religions and then the sciences continued to exert their influence over the populations of Eurasia, and eventually of the entire world, shaping the lives and cultures of human beings everywhere.

Did the short circuit caused by the encounter of these two timescales, of politics and religion, produce a hot spot, as in Mexico, where the life of the earth coincided with that of history to knock palace, pyramid, and cathedral out of balance?

* *Note*: This section was written long before the catastrophic fire that devastated Notre-Dame de Paris in April 2019.

Multiple Clocks

The clock that measures the duration of history, riddled with politics and the fate of empires, obeys neither the same rhythm nor, above all, the same tempo as the one that marks the time of the rites, myths, and behaviors inspired by beliefs, still less the one of living creatures undergoing evolution, still less again that of the earth and of the tectonic plates whose movements transform it—hence the many questions that arise concerning time and duration, which is to say their measurement and, more than this, their nature.

My book *L'Incandescent* (2003) begins by adopting a local perspective. The setting is a farmhouse in the Alps, in front of which a little girl is playing with a doll. Purchased in the neighboring village, the toy lasts for a few weeks; the child has celebrated her sixth birthday; her grandparents have just blown out eighty candles; the building and its walls have held up the roof for four centuries; the sheep, the cattle, and the pigs were domesticated in the Neolithic, at the same time that floral species appeared; the mountain's folding occurred in the Tertiary; the sun that illuminates it will explode in four billion years . . . Time is layered in local space. But is it the same time in each case? How is it to be counted?

I am not writing these lines at the same tempo as the farmer plows the furrows of his field; the prime numbers do not appear at the same tempo as the whole numbers, though they are produced by them; amoebae do not divide and mutate at the same tempo as dinosaurs and humans reproduce . . . Did glaciers carve out the valleys of the Andes, the Alps, and Himalayas at the same tempo as the sea traces out its sentences on the coastlines carved out from Brittany and Ireland? Do the tectonic plates shift at the same tempo as the universe expands? Does the weather change at the same tempo as the lunatic whims of Marianne in Alfred de Musset's play?

I therefore consider it impossible to measure the rhythms, tempos, and durations of religions and empires using a single time-counter, since they do not evolve at the same rate or by means of analogous transformations; religions are millennial and, notwithstanding small changes, virtually invariant; empires are secular and intensely volatile. One clock would measure the ultraslow advance of the subterranean plates that carry the continents, another the evolution of living species, and so on. The times measured by these devices may occasionally coincide, of course, but their alignments are sudden, unexpected, unpredictable. In the case of volcanic eruptions, earthquakes, tsunamis, and the like, two or more clocks may abruptly strike on the same date: the disaster of Lisbon, famines, nuclear winter . . .

The Trajectory of Hot Spots

We must therefore record time with the aid of at least six different clocks, stacked on top of one another, as it were. One of them is universal and spans billions of years, the whole of the grand narrative, from the Big Bang until the present day; another evolutionary, also spanning billions of years, in which species appear, flourish, and die; another, spanning millions of years, measures the life of the human race from its hominid origins; the pendulum of another, religious and millennial, begins to swing back and forth at the dawn of the axial age. With this last clock I also count out the years of the sciences, since geometry, stable on the whole except for small variations, has endured since the time of its invention, now for almost thirty centuries; also the years of artistic masterpieces, since the *Odyssey*, the works of Phidias and

Praxiteles, certain African masks, *Don Quixote*, and Mozart's concertos have not aged in the course of time.

Yet another clock, historical and secular, tracks the rise and fall of fragile empires. And there is a last clock, mine and yours, whose hours and days and months can be read off from the watches that we wear on our wrists, from now until the moment of our death. Why does history, as it is usually written, limit itself to chronicling only one or another of these spans?

The Hot Spot of the Present

The times counted out by these clocks converge on a single point: now. Can one really conceive of historical time without taking into account a line that traverses the others, from the longest ages, measured in billions of years, to the shortest ones, measured in days? Caught up in our parochial pursuits, so often cruel to the point of abomination, why do we forget the grand rhythms of the universe, of the earth, of knowledge and of fate, all of which, as I have shown, begin in and are read through a scripture? Can the intersections between these times, these hot spots, sometimes burning, always decisive, transform our view of history?

Can we actually conceive of the evolution of life without taking into account the billions of years that came before and made possible the emergence of duplicators from lifeless molecules? That the early stages of the universe preceded the appearance of living creatures, improbable though their origin may have been, could not have helped but influence the manner of their birth, their development, and their disappearance, by subjecting them to the implacable laws of physics and chemistry. That the evolution of life preceded, by an immensely long interval, the appearance of hominids could not have helped but influence the emergence of learning and culture, among animals to begin with, and eventually among human communities. So too the progressive and suddenly multiple formation of diverse cultures preceded, by millions of years, the invention of writing, and therefore of recorded history; this invention could not have failed to be affected by what came before. What is more, over a large part of the world, the axial age witnessed the emergence of behaviors that we recognize as religious and that remained stable for thousands of years, whereas history, as it is usually written, charts local fluctuations in political and social life over the same period. Human history, as we are accustomed to think of it, cannot remain indifferent to history itself. The link between all these ages, where what came before again and again shaped what came after, does not obey the logical law *post hoc ergo propter hoc*; it is not, in other words, a strictly causal link. What we are dealing with here are real, yet fuzzy and often obscure statistical correlations that are all the harder to detect as they come from a distant past.

Time and Tempo

In discussing time at some length, I have used three words over and over: duration, rhythm, and tempo. Music distinguishes the last two. Rhythm repeats a single proportion. Any waltz, slow or fast, constantly dances in three-quarter time, which can be played *adagio, andante, allegro, prestissimo*, and so on; variable tempos are associated with a fixed rhythm. The inverted pendulum rod of a metronome, like the pendulum of a clock, keeps a steady beat, the rhythm; the adjustable weight on the rod sets the tempo. Two ways of measuring time.

So it is too with the world of things. Rhythm provides the framework for everything there is, but the tempo of the galaxies differs from that of the planets, still more from that of crystals, and still more again from that of living creatures. The life of mayflies passes *presto* by comparison with that of human beings, which passes *allegro* by comparison with that of sequoias.

Clock and Metronome

In order to measure time, then, we need to abandon the clock in favor of the metronome. The metronome follows the ticktock of the pendulum clock, writ large on its dial in accordance with a quasi-nycthemeral rhythm having a base of six or twelve. From the point of view of rhythm alone, a clock is a metronome; both devices use rhythm to analyze time. But the clock suffers from a crippling disadvantage: it does not mark the tempo. The sliding weight on the rod of the metronome, by contrast, permits it to vary the tempo in a continuous manner.

Once one measures time by means of a metronome, once one considers a clock to be a partial metronome, once one conceives of time as a synthesis of rhythm and tempo, then everything becomes clear. My life is shorter than that of the planet, but its tempo is entirely different: earth and water revolve slowly, I move and think rapidly. Like mornings and tides, pulse and respiration succeed one another in two-beat time, the former *adagio*, the latter *vivace*; a flu virus mutates *presto*, whereas the tempo of the mutations that produced human beings is majestically *andante*. Might one say, then, that I have witnessed as many events as the sea or a virus, only in a more compressed fashion? That, as a matter of physiology, my spoken words, my thoughts, outpace my lungs and my heart? Some people live intensely, others take it easy. Are my own somatic tempos added together, laid on top of one another, as those of the world, of matter, and of other living creatures are? Do human beings experience as many events as galaxies, which are almost as old as the universe, or, on shorter scales, oceans, sequoias, and whales, only, by comparison with them, *allegretto* or *prestissimo*? If I were not part of this larger community, how would I know them? Why would I love them? All of us, whether inert, living, or *sapiens*, we adhere to one another like strata laid on top of one another.

Being and Time

Everything that exists has the same rhythm; each living being has a different tempo, which is to say a different frequency. The first is universal and makes it possible to conserve existence, since by its very nature it resists entropy. For the rhythm—ticktock, two-beat time—is an elementary order, the simplest one there is. If it is interrupted, a spinning top falls over; if not, a rotating gyroscope stays on course, the more rapid the rotation the better; interfere with their rhythm and they begin to wobble every which way. In the absence of order there is only emptiness, disorganization, chaos, and immobility; no more time, no more being. Once rhythm disappears, existence melts away into randomness, disorder, and death.

Tempo, for its part, makes all manner of material existence singular, atoms and molecules, living creatures, species and individuals, organs and tissues, you and me. Time depends on circumstance: rhythm writes down its stanzas as an eternal recurrence; tempo is a matter of frequency, which distinguishes persons and things from one another.

Rhythm is a closed circle; tempo is various and open. Resisting entropy, rhythm responds to the question: why is there something rather than nothing? Answer: because everything that exists is periodic. In varying the ways of opposing entropy, tempo satisfies the principle of individuation: this exists rather than that.

Who am I? The synthesis of many tempos, which arrange their frequencies harmonically and cram them into the existence of my body. Health or sickness? The harmony or disharmony of this synthesis. Death? The analysis, or decomposition, of this synthesis. I find the idea of representing death as a flat electroencephalogram all the more pleasing as it defines all existence with reference to a periodic function, even if a complex and chaotic one, as if flatness marked the end of its vibrations. Stop the beating and you are left with disorder, randomness, death, inexistence. Everything that exists battles against entropy, each living being resists it in its own way. Rhythm is essential and universal, tempo is existential and singular. Rhythm is the same in all things, each one has its own tempo; everything that exists is rhythmic, each living being vibrates with its own frequency. Open your ears to the rotations of the tides, of the planets, stars, seasons, DNA, musical chords . . . Colors and sounds, your sensations, idle chatter, music—your signals vibrate with their vibrations.

Everything is number, everything is *arithmos*? No, everything is *rhythmos*.

Let the adjustable weight of the metronome move continuously along its rod and you will realize that there are as many singular individuals as there are points on a line—the transfinite fortune of living beings! Neither the pendulum clock nor the stopwatch can or knows how to show this—whence the many errors that philosophers make in conceiving of time in terms of a flat number line (Kant and the series of natural numbers), or of duration in terms of increasing entropy (Bergson waiting for a cube of sugar to dissolve).

The clock turns out to be a poor machine for measuring time, then, since it has at its disposal only two tempos: the frequency of the pendulum, rapidly ticking off the seconds, and the slower frequency of the dial, whose hands pass though the hours of the day and night, following the rotation of our planet. The metronome is far superior, for it can indicate all possible frequencies.

Our disagreements, mistakes, misconceptions, and misunderstandings flow from this existential jumble of different frequencies. It is a miracle when I encounter friendship or love as lively as mine! Yes, a miracle, because the immense multiplicity of frequencies, the coexistence of these various tempos, ought to lead every moment to the most intense dissonance. No one has ever played *adagio* and *presto* together. The difficulty of knowing and loving has its source in this disorder. And yet I exist as the summation or synthesis of all the different tempos of my organs and functions; the earth, the world, the universe itself exist as the result of agreements and compromises among billions of frequencies. For if each tempo singularizes heart, lung, and liver, all of them must somehow cooperate as parts of a unified organism. Health is agreement among frequencies; madness and sickness, scatterings. Whether galaxy, storm, or little girl, all are Fourier series. Impossible to define or to sum up, life and the universe hold this multiplicity together, keeping cacophony at bay by harmonizing discordant elements. Bottom line: you and I, living creatures, earth and sky, let us, rhythmic beings all, let us bind things together, to one another, by virtue of the continuity that unites the singular series of our frequencies.

Mimicking the World

This is what religion does, in its Roman Catholic expression. Like the universe, life, and the world, it binds things together, living creatures and human beings. In the winter, Christmas; in the spring, Easter, whose date was determined by calculating the epact in order to align the rhythms of the sun and the moon. These festivals mimic the rhythm of the seasons and the years, their various frequencies. In the same way, religion mimics the stages of a life: the conception, birth, and death of Christ, all commemorated. By means of the sacraments it relates the times of our lives to one another: baptism at the beginning, confirmation in adolescence, marriage in adulthood, extreme unction as death draws near. It does this, too, by means of rites: the common mass of everyday worship, the special services reserved for the holiest days; psalms, litanies, the rosary; also liturgical signs, the liturgy of the Word, spoken or prayed, and so on. Mimicking the rhythm of the world, religion binds together its tempos.

The Catholic monastery amounts to a scale model, a compact summary of all religions, and in this again it mimics the world, life, and the human body. Matins and lauds; prime, tierce, sext, and none; vespers, compline—all these prayers mark the canonical hours of the day, major and minor, every day of the year; all these prayers express the monastery's adamant resolve to close itself off from the space around it, even from space itself, in order to unify this rhythmic pattern, making it more dense, so that time itself, as it passes and flows, vanishes and gives way to a primordial periodic order.

A decisive moment in the struggle against entropy! And
so we are brought back to our old puteal, whose round chimney opens up to anyone who embraces this way of rhythmi-
cally marking time, from prime to compline, from vespers
to matins—a foretaste of eternity. This hot spot, local, well
delineated, traverses the tempos of the world.

Two hot spots, to be exact, one Christian, the other
pagan. The Lord's prayer begins with the words "Our Father,
who art in heaven . . ." Here "Father" speaks of procreation;
"our" refers to a community; "heaven" covers the world.
In six words this hot spot bridges, traverses, binds living
creatures together into a collectivity, reasserts their common
rhythm and associates their various tempos with one another.
In the same way, by his name alone, Jupiter united the day
and the father, the world and life; bound the external to the
personal, the natural to the cultural.

Line of Hot Spots

In order to estimate the magnitude of religious energy, I have
chosen the image of tectonic plates, less to contrast what lies
on the surface with what lies below than to give a sense of
depth to the innumerable tempos of living beings. Like the
tectonic plates of history, some moving slowly, others quickly,
religion links us, in a continuous motion, to the grand narrative of the world, to all the rhythmic beatings of matter and
living beings, earth and heaven, water and fire; links all of us
to one another. By its tempo, religion assures a fluid transition
between the universal and the singular; it is divine, because it
goes beyond us and provides us with a foundation; human,
because it does not cease to act upon us—by which I mean
that it causes the ground beneath our feet to move. Religion
connects my heart with the tides of the ocean, my lungs with

the mountains, my hunger with the earth, my emotions with seismic tremors, the fire of volcanos and stars with the heat of my limbs, my genitals, and my feelings; its burning plate connects my loved ones and my friends with others, connects my life with the fate of the world and of humanity.

Chimney of the Present

I come back now to the times counted out on each metronome: they are directed toward now and here, in me and outside of me, and point the way there like the opening of a chimney, through which the smoke of a thousand tempos swirls. Every day I forget my carbon atoms and the electrostatic attraction that holds them together, allowing me to run and jump. The gestures of chimpanzees, my cousins, which I happen to imitate without knowing it, may sometimes come to mind, like Lucy's somewhat rolling gait; more often the roots of my language and the fascinating criminal rites of human sacrifice resurface in my consciousness. I have a clearer recollection of the storming of the Bastille, commemorated in France every year in the month of July; the events of my childhood frequently come back to memory. Thus I can drill through the present, the way glaciologists core ice sheets; on the sample extracted from these depths I detect layers in strata that are increasingly distant from the surface, each of which follows one of these tempos, reaching an end point that is all the more deeply buried the longer time has gone on. The further time goes back, the slower it is, the more universal; the closer it comes to the surface, the more rapid it is, the more singular.

But this burial in a darker and darker oblivion does not signify a growing insignificance, quite to the contrary. I would be nothing, I would not be able to think or act, history itself would be no more substantial than the wind if these subterranean times did not constitute a solid and lasting foundation; without matter, heat, energy, earth, life, hominization, and rites, without the whole of their laws and arrangements, neither collective history nor personal existence would be possible.

Reading time from a metronome tells us about temporal evolution on a global scale, continually being pushed forward, ceaselessly being resumed and reiterated; an evolution whose stupendous and layered span transports successive states while molding them in its immense flux, an unpredictable and irregular torrent that bifurcates and reaches unexpected shores, differently formed, to be sure, according to their own tempos, but by a route likewise exhibiting a constant rhythm.

We can neither think nor act as if we were not made of matter; as if we were not living creatures, to begin with, then animals; as if, still later, we had not inherited behaviors and thoughts inscribed in our deep cultural memory; in short, as if we were not, still today, religious, social, and political animals, devoted to this other world that the grand narrative shapes and encounters. We live, I live in and through these worlds, multiple and shimmering, issuing—we still do not know how—from this interminable narrative, source of the objective, the collective, the cognitive, the subjective of our own time. These tempos, piled on top of one another, make it possible to generalize Darwinian evolution to the universe as a whole. I am, we are material, living, cultural, religious, historical, personal. All this hangs together; all this is bound together; all this is reread together—only now reading from the adjustable weight of the metronome rather than the dial or the pendulum of a clock.

Now this well, this chimney burrows through the ground beneath me. Am I a puteal? Am I a hot spot?

Apprehending the Objective World
Where in this stack of tempos is the plate whose beating pulse is peculiar to religion—and to science? I see it as lying above the Darwinian plate of natural history where plant and animal species first appear and, more proximately, above the one where hominization begins to flourish, heralding the emergence of political life and the establishment of cities and social groups. I see it, in other words, as conditioned by what came before and conditioning what came after—and therefore decisive for the formation and development of modern human cultures, in all their variety.

Now, as far as I know, all the plates except the one bearing the religious domain contain real, which is to say earthly tempos, whereas through religion the celestial tempos of another world echo forth. Virtual, formal, sometimes eternal, this other world functions as a means of binding the objective, the collective, the emotive, and the subjective to the cognitive, as though in a colossal embrace. Myths and religions, each in their own way, relate the origin of the world and the appearance of living creatures, first, then of human beings, telling of their destinies and the meaning of their lives, of their communities, of their history, of their personal intimacies; that is, they connect all these plates with one another.

This link, this relation, node, or seam, this integration, suture, or ligature, this universality acts as a sort of matrix (again, in the geological sense), a sort of synthesis; in short, as a pulsating jet of immense force—precisely because it is capable of passing through all the plates, with a constant rhythm, and yet, being various, with a changeable tempo.

If this vertical emission can be separated into its compo-
nent parts and purified, purged of its emotive, collective,
and subjective aspects, it will be possible to arrive at a novel
cognitive perspective in which the objective world can be
fully apprehended and acted on.

Events, Imaginary and Otherwise

The visit of the Three Wise Men, the manger scene of
Christmas night, and the eucharistic revelation of the Last
Supper on the evening of Maundy Thursday are considered by most historians to be imaginary events, made out
of whole cloth by fervent disciples unconcerned with fac-
tual accuracy. Who would doubt this conclusion? Myself, I
trust the historians. Similarly, no one—as far as I know—
believes in the story of Thales's calculations at the foot of
the pyramids or of Hippasus's drowning, punishment for
having discovered the irrational numbers. The idea that
Etna's eruption threw up Empedocles's sandal, following
his suicide, makes the hypercritically minded laugh, and
not without reason.

If, however, one looks at these events as parts of a whole,
as I have done; if one reexamines the eucharistic revelation,
seeing it instead as the final revision of a millennial law concerning sacrifice, the last stage in a cycle that, having passed
from the ritual offering of a human being to that of an animal, culminated in the manducation of a wafer, something
obtained not from fauna but from flora (more about this
later)—then we are dealing with hot spots in which the brisk
tempo of history is superimposed on the tempos of religion
and rigorous knowledge. Suddenly, history, religion, and
knowledge interfere with one another.

A Conundrum

What, then, are we to say about something that is not a proven fact, a documented event, but a myth, a story having no historical basis, which is therefore neither true nor false, or so hypercritical historians would argue, but which is nonetheless endowed with a depth as unfathomable as that of a volcanic chimney and an influence as long-lasting as the interval between a volcano's eruption and the cooling of its lava? How is it, in other words, that the effects of an event that never took place can reverberate on a millennial scale? Here we are confronted by something more important, at least in its various commemorations, than a decisive historical moment, whether a military victory or the enthronement of a king.

We will never celebrate the fall of Rome or the devastation wrought by Attila. But many of us pray every morning, in the silence of chapels throughout the world, the smallest and most humble not least among them, in obedience to a sacrament, the Eucharist, that has no historical substance. Many Latin countries celebrate the Feast of the Epiphany, no matter that the Magi may never have existed or visited the manger; mathematicians around the world go on calculating and proving theorems, no matter that the Pythagoreans may never have existed.

How can something that is almost nothing have so much influence? Simply for this reason: it holds everything together, like a conductor who, by his gestures, unifies the various instruments and sections of an orchestra.

Legends or Facts?

What, at bottom, is a historical fact? Is it an actual event, something that really happened, which long ago may have changed the world but which everyone apart from a few scholars has now forgotten? Or is it also a vague, persistent, undying legend that has long compelled the belief of multitudes, a pure fabrication whose impact has nonetheless made itself felt down through the centuries? The battle of Salamis delivered the Greeks from Persian domination. But what remains of these two powers? Scipio destroyed Carthage and Rome ruled in its place. But what is left of these two empires? Of the axial age, by contrast, everything survives virtually unchanged; in the case of geometry, only a few lines have moved.

The term "legend," in the positive sense given it by a decorative emblem at the bottom of maps, indicates how they are to be read, how what they represent is to be understood. It is in this sense that the image of hot spots and of a chimney, linking up tempos by means of a vertical embrace, belongs to the legend of centuries and millennia. This sort of explanation, even though it is widely ridiculed, often has greater weight in our cultural life and what we do every day than duly documented historical facts.

Myths are what link religion and science, both of which occupy lower strata than the one occupied by superficial history, and enable us to reread their strange legends (in the usual sense of the word), in order to decipher them, in the same way that earlier we tried to detect the main stanzas of the grand narrative.

Philosophy of History

Let us now come back to the question of time and tectonic shifts. How does the deepest plate, broad and slow-moving, carry along the historical continents whose temporal variousness it has supported for so long?

The ancient Greeks, having only a circular conception of time, did not think of history as being irreversible in the modern sense. The prophets of Israel, and those who wrote down their prophecies, invented the idea of irreversibility for two reasons. First, because their purpose was to announce the future. Little by little, God was realized in and through the destiny of a chosen people. No other nation seems to have anticipated its future in this way. Time therefore became meaningful. This led on to a second motivation. In thinking about time, it was not enough, as Kant supposed, to arrange numbers on a line. A more comprehensive conception was needed, more ordinal than cardinal. And this undertaking, irreversible to the Hebrew mind, had a name: the Messiah. The Jews, the chosen people, awaited him; the Christians, in their turn, recognized him in the person of Christ and likewise awaited his return. That God was realized in the destiny of the people he had chosen filled time with meaning during the interval; that this same people awaited the Messiah gave them an aim and an end. Here, then, is the deep plate, the deepest of all, the first philosophy of history—a religious philosophy. It has a meaning, by virtue of the constancy of its rhythm.

A new link, a new ligature, was dreamt by the Italian theologian Joachim of Fiore. In a first age, according to the Old Testament, God the Father created the world; in a second, according to the Gospels, his Son came down to it. We are now awaiting, Joachim maintained, the advent of a third era, the Age of the Holy Spirit, since Christ lived, announced the Good News, died, was resurrected, disappeared. Thus the medieval monk from Calabria overlaid secular duration with the dogma of the Trinity. He was a dreamer, as I say, as everyone says. And yet he linked up everything.

The fact remains that, since Joachim, no philosophy of history, whether theistic or atheistic, spiritual or materialistic, precise, fanciful, imaginary, or scientific, has lacked this tripartite division or failed to project into the future the reign of the spirit, a pacific utopia and classless society. Dating the beginnings of a more peaceful age from the present time, I confess I have yielded myself to this tradition, with its three tempos. In a learned and carefully documented study, the Jesuit theologian Henri de Lubac demonstrated the permanence, the broad invariance that obtains despite slight variations—a robust messianism that was influential from the Middle Ages to the time of Pascal and Bossuet, persisting during the Enlightenment and later in the thought of Hegel and Marx, it has come down through the centuries to our own day. Philosophy of history attaches itself to the vertical plate of religions linking together various tempos. For none of the horizontal plates we have considered is capable of so encompassing an embrace.

Gloria

Innumerable generations, for centuries and centuries, have chanted the final verse of the rites and recitatives of Christianity in its various denominations, *Gloria Patri, et Filio, et Spiritui Sancto* (Glory be to the Father, and to the Son, and to the Holy Spirit); but have they also meditated no less diligently on the phrase that follows this praise, *sicut erat in principio et nunc et semper et in saecula saeculorum* (as it was in the beginning, is now, and ever shall be, world without end), whose statement unfurls time from its origin and ever thereafter? Distinct and separate, these two acclamations, the one singing the praises of the Trinity, the other describing the totality of times while integrating them, are conjoined and conjugated by means of a single word: in English "as," in Latin *sicut*. Were the innumerable generations who sang these acclamations aware of the impossibility of this likeness, this *sicut*? For it does not go without saying that eternity, however fragmented it may be, is distributed, is scattered throughout time.

And yet these generations solemnly affirmed that the Trinity is conjugated, that it is conjoined with the duration of the world, of living creatures and human beings. Does the Trinity name this duration, does it resemble it? Yes, it is *like* it, *sicut*. Does the Latin conjunction put the two things into contact with each other? Yes, the Trinity, though eternal, develops in time, or, more precisely, develops time, as if it sums it up and punctuates it, as if it links the moments of time, ties them together, in a triple embrace. The Trinity is as time is, *sicut*; time is as the Trinity is, resembles it. And, like the Trinity, duration unfolds in three terms: God at the beginning, the incarnate Christ now, the Holy Spirit soon and for ever more: *three individuals for a single person, three existences for a single being; three tempos for a single time.* The Trinity is therefore expressed and can be read in the grand narrative of the universe of things and the evolution of living creatures, whether in the beginnings of the world; now, in the mortal history of Christ and of human beings; always, for the Holy Spirit never ceases to invent, to create bifurcations, to cause novelty to emerge, to encourage us to think, as much in the development of inanimate things and living beings as in the events of history. The constant intervention of the Trinity in time makes all of us the "nows" of hot spots. Did Joachim of Fiore draw his inspiration from this acclamation, twice ternary and each time linked together term by term?

As mysterious as this *sicut* may seem, the fact remains that it translates, transmits, transports eternity into particular moments of time, as if eternity poured its intensity into them. The hot spot of a fugitive and fragile now shines and burns with an eternal flame. How can this be? Can we ever know how eternal transcendence descends like lightning into the minute instants of immanence?

Nevertheless, contemplating this ardent mirror, time as the mobile image of eternity; contemplating this junction, this conjunction, this comparison, this reflection, this hyphen, this link, this gullet, this conduit, this narrow channel, this chimney, this passage, this corridor, this raging torrent, this cataract, this blazing flash of lightning whose blinding short circuit brings the contingent and the immutable into contact—doing this exposes existence to ecstasy.

Birth, Ecstasy, Night

God hides himself in deepest darkness, as much in the night of the world, which the world wishes not to understand, as in the unbelief of my soul and the ignorance of my reason, crushed by the contradictions concerning my existence; in the dark mystery, too, that awaits me after death. God has withdrawn into these obscurities.

Before me, as it happens, someone living in the West in the twenty-first century, having enough money to eat, drink, and keep warm, someone who has some small mastery of learning and language, there shines, weakly, a star, flickering against this somber background. I am this star, and at the end of a journey that will last the length of my life, I finally come, not in the light of a sun-drenched noon, outside a Platonic cave, but during the night, to a dark stable; inside, in a manger, in the company of beasts and shepherds, an infant wails, his father on one side, his mother, who has just given birth, on the other; in the darkness they can scarcely be seen.

And so I begin to understand that night is not only the model of knowledge, but the model of birth. Everything begins in darkness—the *noche oscura* of Saint John of the Cross—the minute and the locally isolated. The light of the star fades in the early dawn, not yet bright. Everything begins very small, from the infantile babbling that leads on to language, from abject poverty to wealth, from pastoral ignorance to applied knowledge, from a seed to a leafy tree, from the infinitesimal beating of a butterfly's wings to a great storm, from an almost nonexistent potential to the reality of new worlds, from a subtle inspiration to a new poem or theorem, from an absent abstraction to the explanation of a present universe, from an empathy whose goodness extends from my brother, wounded, lying in a ditch, to humanity itself—this gospel comes down to me without law, order, precept, or rule, in a disparate and fortunate abundance, a dazzling cataract, unilluminated by epiphany. Born of an infinitesimal burning point, this aurora of beatitudes, this starry night with billions of galaxies and constellations—atoms and worlds, cells and organisms, notes and musics, letters and languages, elements and systems, axioms and geometries, individuals and groups, the ones bound up with the others in the embrace I mentioned—connecting with the infinite, like apexes and summits, the web of the universe, all these things transport us, fill us with ecstasy. *Coeli et terra enarrent universa mirabilia tua*: the heavens and earth relate your universal wonders.

Alas, this superabundant and profuse clarity can utterly vanish once again into the blackest darkness—the darkness, for example, in which savages take up arms and massacre innocents. In order to protect this improbable birth, this wailing of one who is always newborn, from a violence whose obstinate energy, ever-recurring, was later to condemn him to torment and agony, to save this sudden mutation from ruthless elimination by the surrounding society, Jesus's parents flee, taking him to Egypt, a country that the Jews compared at the time to Sheol, a hell of blind and deadly darkness, where God, then and always *absconditus*, resides and hides himself. Once again, God withdraws and I see no one.

King deprived of all power, magus innocent of all knowledge, I must go back to wandering.

CHAPTER 2

HORIZONTAL BINDING

Genesis of Bonds

Along a vertical axis, religion links heaven with earth, transcendence with immanence, in an immense embrace. Religion also links human beings to one another, along a horizontal axis, to form groups, assemblies, and processions. The hot spot at the intersection of these two dimensions Christianity calls the Incarnation. To put it another way: in Christianity, the communion of saints associates the two; from the first derive the hard sciences, from the second the human sciences.

The preceding chapter moves as fast as the lightning that strikes from on high; the present chapter advances slowly, like a tide spreading over a broad beach. Two tempos. The first part of the book, *allegro*; the second, *andante*.

Saint Peter's Tears

I begin by inquiring into the manner in which social groups come to be formed. On a park bench two lovers kiss, nobody pays any attention. Two louts get into an argument, yelling and waving their arms, many people pay attention. If a serious accident occurs, leaving the victims covered in blood, everyone stops and stares. Violence and death bind people together. Tragedy is their passion. The media exploit this tendency, nourishing it with cadavers and death on a daily basis.

But the power of laughter to recruit and unite the members of a group, often a very large group, should not be underestimated. I only partly distinguish the comic from the tragic, since spiteful and demeaning laughter can be no less lethal than unbridled violence. Amiable and gentle laughter, by contrast, with its soothing affability, can be a source of moral instruction; indeed, using laughter of this kind to expose and correct ethical shortcomings is a venerable tradition, from the commedia dell'arte of sixteenth-century Italy until the present day, including my own recent collection of essays, *Morales espiègles* (2019). Comedy fills as many seats in the theater as tragedy.

After considering the way in which small groups form, often in the course of a violent spectacle in which someone is sentenced to die, let us then raise our point of view to take in a larger audience, the crowd. Finally, from a still greater height, let us look upon a map of the world and humanity itself.

To begin with, a small assembly, a sort of tribunal:

Now Peter was sitting outside in the courtyard. And a maid came up to him, and said, "You also were with Jesus the Galilean." But he denied it before them all, saying, "I do not know what you mean." And when he went out to the porch, another maid saw him, and she said to the bystanders, "This man was with Jesus of Nazareth." And again he denied it with an oath, "I do not know the man." After a little while the bystanders came up and said to Peter, "Certainly you are also one of them, for your accent betrays you." Then he began to invoke a curse on himself and to swear, "I do not know the man." And immediately the cock crowed. And Peter remembered the saying of Jesus, "Before the cock crows, you will deny me three times." And he went out and wept bitterly.

Matthew 26:69–75

A more dramatic version of the same scene is found in Luke 22:55–62, which relates that a fire had been kindled in the courtyard: in the glow of the flames, a servant girl recognized Peter.

Peter's denial, recounted in each of the Gospels (almost identically in the synoptics, more succinctly in John), reminds us of a human, all too human moment of the Passion. A painful episode that has often been portrayed by artists, in the paintings of Caravaggio and Rembrandt, in the poems of Baudelaire, in the motets of Charpentier.

Before a Fire at Night

Having left his family and home, Peter followed his master at a distance, a lost soul who came finally to a courtyard; inside the high priest's house a tribunal was convened, where iniquity would judge innocence. Bewildered, in the company of a few servants who were warming themselves before a fire they had made, he sat down. From the moment he uttered his first words, shivering with the others in the cold night, Peter the apostle, head of the saints, cornerstone of the future Church, denied Christ.

Although he had been forewarned, long ago, he nonetheless denied Christ three times. Yet no one had threatened him; a servant girl merely asked him a question; then another girl inquired of him, in the same way; perhaps, as in Matthew's account, someone scorned him, as so many people have mocked me in the past: your accent gives you away! Then, honest though he was, he lied; pure, he defiled himself; holy, he damned himself. Seeking to forestall malicious laughter, fearing ridicule, he denied.

Does this story show Peter's weakness, his sinfulness, as is usually supposed? I am inclined to resist this interpretation.

Two Tribunals

First, let us look closely at the group gathered around the fire, outside, in the darkness of night. The synoptic account constitutes a sort of scale model, simple, popular, external, but obscure, of what went on inside, in the house, where Jesus, both man and God, confronted the assembly of the powerful of this world alone, under the bright light of torches. It is altogether as though, in this place, there sat not one, but two courts of justice: the one grand, official, legal, the Sanhedrin; the other small, improvised, scarcely visible in the weak light of the flickering flames.

Here, a person of excellent character, destined to hold high offices, only now friendless, alone in the darkness, encountered a small group of humble people warming themselves before the fire, gossiping and talking about the latest news. One has the sense that the grand scene of judgment unfolding inside was being repeated on a minor scale, before a spontaneous popular tribunal, a primitive kind of jury. We are feeling our way along to the source we are seeking, the origin of social groups. Their beginnings are hard to make out, with only a small fire to dispel the darkness of night.

When one of the servant girls asked him a question and began, as one may imagine, to laugh at his response, Peter, caught in the web, feeling that he himself was being judged, sought refuge in denial. The high court inside sentenced the archetypal scapegoat; the lower court outside caused the embryonic scapegoat to betray.

Weakness? Cowardice? To be sure, Peter denied Christ, there is no doubt of that; but let us continue to suspend judgment, keeping in mind that our censure is no less blinkered than the judgment of a tribunal. Judged in our turn, we are sensitive to an injustice that is committed in private against an upright person. But are we equally sensitive to the same dynamic when it plays out in public, beginning with small things, ordinary words and gestures, with scarcely any hint of aggressiveness, often accompanied by roars of laughter— this in the darkness of a frigid early spring night? Isolated individuals are often scorned in this way. The charge of weakness brought against Peter blinds us to the influence of the group, no matter that it is almost entirely free of violence.

Inside, before the Sanhedrin, a court of justice blinded by violence, an innocent man appeared, advocating peace. Outside, in the courtyard, where servants were huddling around a fire, a scale model of this court, a small improvised tribunal, found another innocent guilty of treachery. Evidently one who denies betrays. But who would dare to challenge a group of accusers by himself? As counsel for the accused, I move to have the verdict overturned.

We readily suppose Peter to be weak and sinful, without taking into account the power of numbers, however small they may be. After the evening meal of Passover, the scapegoat was led through the city to the house of the high priest, to the taunts of a furious crowd; everyone spit upon Jesus. As for Peter, what do you expect him to have done, all alone? Do you wish that he had died, that, like Jesus, he had assumed the role of victim? What would we have done—what would we have said, in his place, in the face of this collective mania? That we knew Christ? We would have risked our lives. Here the guilty party is less Peter than Jerusalem itself, the violence of a society bent on prosecuting Jesus, whether it expressed itself formally, in the language of the high court, the Sanhedrin, or whether it cried out against Peter in the common dialect, the language of the people, among the menials who warmed their hands and faces before the opaque fire in the courtyard.

Observe what happens. At the very moment when a lone individual comes into contact with the web of relations formed by even the smallest gathering, he finds himself, like a fly caught in a spider's web, a prisoner, entangled, ensnared, poisoned, imprisoned. Who was Peter, in and of himself? Perfect, or nearly so; courageous right up to the moment of his death; soon to be the first pope, tortured in the end, again by crucifixion, sanctified later. How and why did so small a group change him so quickly? What power did it contain within itself that it could suddenly bring about such a metamorphosis, that it could turn a faithful disciple, a hero, into a perjurer?

Inside and outside, a man stood alone before an assembly, official in the case of the high court, informal in the case of the lower one. Below, a small group transformed an apostle into a traitor; above, a large group transformed a just man into a guilty man. In both cases the group posed a similar question. Who are you? A provincial, a man from Galilee?

The Messiah, the King of the Jews? One of his associates? Yes, you have been seen with him.

From the scale model in the courtyard to the divine Passion, collective variation extends from a gathering of humble people to the august judges of the Sanhedrin—thus the whole of society is passed through, from top to bottom, in accordance with the same dynamic by which it was brought into being. Individual variation, for its part, extends from the sinner to the Incarnate, from a man to a god, from a traitor to an innocent. Above, the model; below, its copy, on a smaller scale. The grand spectacle of the Sanhedrin is reproduced, in the courtyard, as a lower, popular sort of court-martial, disguised by the good-natured (or at least not unfriendly) manner of its members. Or rather: the servants, in questioning Peter, unwittingly reveal how courts of justice came to be constituted in the first place. The scale model shows us a tribunal in its primitive state. This is a question not only of resemblance, by reason of similarity, but also of a genesis, through evolution. The grand spectacle of judgment does no more than throw into relief and magnify what happens every day in our conversations with others, our little chitchats. Death roams among us. Does it make this "us"?

Let us pause here for a moment and try to think further about this search for the guilty, conducted by tribunals, but secretly born in the hearts of human beings, obsessed with the problem of evil. Who is guilty, they ask, who is responsible for evil? Could it be, I ask, that evil—which is to say violence—is at the very root of social groups? In order to answer these questions, we must imagine, not one, but three types of tribunals.

The first is the usual type of tribunal, the one that we all know. Defendants are found guilty or innocent of crimes or misdemeanors, under aggravating or extenuating circumstances, following argument and the verdict of a judge or a jury, and so sentenced or acquitted. There is nothing new here, we know how this kind of justice functions. We have just seen two versions of it, on a large and a small scale. Something else is needed.

A Second Tribunal

I therefore am led to imagine a second kind of tribunal—never before convened, and for good reason—before which could be summoned to appear the societies that have populated the planet in the past and those that populate it today, historical and prehistorical both, great and small alike, weak and strong: crowds, families, social classes, towns, cities, nations, states, empires, as well as the small group, the scale model of the Sanhedrin itself, assembled in the courtyard before a dying fire—in short, societies of all types. This tribunal, as I say, has never been established, has never been named, has never been conceived, since we always judge in the name of society.

The customary arrangement now having been stood on its head, the new court poses the following question to the societies appearing before it: what one among you has never manufactured armaments, provoked conflicts, made war, mistreated women and trampled the poor underfoot, exercised arbitrary powers and instituted futile hierarchies, and, consequently, committed cruel injustices; what one among you has not overabundantly killed, even within families, even among brothers? What society has not celebrated its history as one of killers—Achilles, Joshua, Scipio, Horatius and Caesar, Roland, El Cid, Louis XIV, Napoleon, Joffre, Rommel . . .—without considering for a moment how many people have died at their hands? Let a lawyer come forward and show that even one society has been innocent of these crimes. Let a historian, a prehistorian, an ethologist, an anthropologist come forward. They will have to confess that we do not know of a single one.

Transhistorical evidence: none. Why has the force of so damning a conclusion never been acknowledged? Simply because, from one age to the next, societies transmit to posterity innumerable accounts meant to ignore the plain facts of the matter, to exculpate themselves of all misdoing— accounts that prevent such a tribunal from being convened in the first place. Excepting perhaps the lamentations of the Old Testament prophets, perhaps the words of the Gospels.

Thanks to these words, we understand why it is, for example, that of every ten stories published by newspapers, radio, and television, the media in general, at least nine involve police reports or detective work of one sort or another in which a guilty party is sought, in which great intelligence and effort are devoted to identifying a criminal. We believe ourselves to be exempt from all blame, whereas for several hours a day, at every meal or before going to bed, we take great pleasure in hearing the tale of a victim and a murderer; we are pleased to wallow in the guilt of others—without ever realizing that, as spectators, we assist the work of a tribunal that judges and sentences an individual while drawing a veil over collective violence. By what right do society and its representatives claim for themselves the right to judge? Why is society itself never put in the dock?

The *Iliad* and *La Chanson de Roland* sing of the bloody exploits of heroic warriors. Who obliges them to die? Their homeland—a lofty and noble maternal figure in the popular imagination, untroubled by moral responsibility; a cruel mother, who requires her sons to give up their lives. What monuments to the dead, what memories of war, will accuse societies of putting millions of their children to death?

We may agree that Peter sinned. But who would dare bring an accusation against the servants huddled around the fire?

The General Solution to the Problem of Evil

I summarize. Verdicts handed down by the first tribunal concern an individual, who is sometimes found guilty, sometimes innocent; the court will decide. Implication: no woman or man is naturally good or evil; that depends on personalities, circumstances, ways of life, DNA, and whatever upbringing and education will make of them. Jesus is found innocent, Peter guilty.

The verdict of the second tribunal, the one I have just called into being: society, not the individual, always bears responsibility for evil.

A Third Tribunal

Finally, and by means of another novelty, the philosopher Leibniz, in the early eighteenth century, summoned to appear, not the Son of God, as the Sanhedrin had done, but God the Father, the Creator himself, before a tribunal that he called Theodicy, on the charge of bearing responsibility for evil. If in fact God created the world, he brought forth in it typhoons, volcanic eruptions, and earthquakes, as well as numberless diseases. Judged in absentia, he too will be found innocent or guilty, in accordance with the pleadings of philosophers, lawyers, and accusers.

How will this third tribunal rule? Will it determine that God is generous or cruel, good or evil? The answer to this apparently undecidable question does not depend, as is usually supposed, on a particular philosophy, on faith or atheism. It involves something else, as I will now try to show.

The Lisbon Earthquake

Recall what Voltaire said regarding the earthquake that struck Lisbon during the Enlightenment. All the philosophers of the age spoke out in the aftermath of the giant tsunami that crashed into the Portuguese coast on 1 November 1755 at 9:40 a.m. Recent calculations place the magnitude of the earthquake that caused it at more than 8.5 on the Richter scale. In combination, the tremor and the vast wall of water that followed in its wake destroyed the city and left more than a hundred thousand people dead. Voltaire spoke for many when he declared that if God had created the world, he would have spared it such a catastrophe, on account of his surpassing goodness. Furthermore, if he created the world, he is also responsible for the evil in it. Thus God was arraigned before another tribunal, not quite a half-century after the one convened by Leibniz. This time he was found guilty.

Here is my argument, opposite to the one made by Voltaire and, I believe, more persuasive. I myself experienced the Loma Prieta earthquake, which shook the San Francisco Bay area on 17 October 1989 at five o'clock in the afternoon, 7.2 on the Richter scale, causing the deaths of more than fifty people. The aftershocks lasted for more than three weeks. The event captured the whole world's attention.

Some years later, in Haiti, a slightly weaker tremor, 7.0, killed more than two hundred thousand people. The power of an earthquake involves the earth, nature, *Deus sive natura*—creation itself, in Voltaire's sense. An earthquake strikes blindly; in the two cases I have just mentioned, the intensity of its shaking near the epicenter was roughly the same, 7.0 as opposed to 7.2. But the tragic difference in the number of victims on these days of wrath, between San Francisco, a rich city, and Haiti, a poor island, depended on the circumstances of the population in the two places, on their degree of social and economic organization, developed or undeveloped, their building codes, their technical and legal resources—in brief, on the political life of a community, more or less well adapted to calamity.

Nature—God, perhaps, at least according to Voltaire and like-minded philosophers—says 7.0 on the Richter scale, or 7.2, a very small difference; politics, history, culture, and the media say two hundred thousand persons dead or fifty, a very great difference. Reckon, decide, judge. Who is responsible? Society. Which is what needed to be demonstrated. The tribunal before which Voltaire summoned God himself to appear has just rendered the opposite verdict. It has found God innocent of such evil.

The second and the third tribunals both issued the same ruling: the guilty party is society. In the face of physically incontestable facts, there can be no doubt that violence is an ineradicably constant feature of human existence. Here lies evil, present in society from the moment of its birth. Once again, a not insignificant judgment.

Must we therefore conclude that Satan governs the great mass of human beings? Let us take our leave of California, Haiti, and Lisbon and come back to the Gospels, or at least to two Gospel texts. First, one dealing with temptation.

Again, the devil took [Jesus] to a very high mountain, and showed him all the kingdoms of the world and the glory of them; and he said to him, "All these I will give you, if you will fall down and worship me." Then Jesus said to him, "Away with you, Satan! . . ."

Matthew 4:8–10

Thus spoke the prince of this world. Here Satan represents the power and the glory of earthly kingdoms.

Among the last words spoken by Christ on the cross are these: "Father, forgive them, for they know not what they do" (Luke 23:34). "They" do not know what "they" do. Who is this indefinite "they," whose sins the Crucified One asks his Father, before breathing his last, to forgive? The plural pronoun designates the soldiers assembled at Golgotha, the crowd that cried, "Free Barabbas," the tribunal that sentenced the innocent. It designates any undifferentiated group, any mass of individuals having no identity separate from membership in the group, that condemns an innocent person to death—in a word, society. Society does not know what it does. It is violent without knowing it. Or, if it does know this, it hides the fact from itself.

Whereas the prophet Jeremiah wept for Jerusalem as a whole, Jesus pardoned individual persons: "Your sins are forgiven," he said. Jesus never condemned an individual person. He pardoned the woman caught in adultery, while rebuking those who, as a group, were eager to punish her: "Let him who is without sin among you be the first to throw a stone at her" (John 8:7).

He pardoned his neighbor on the cross, the Penitent Thief, ignoring the crimes for which a tribunal had sentenced him to the torture of crucifixion: "[T]oday you will be with me in Paradise" (Luke 23:43).

But at Golgotha, like Jeremiah, his lament was reserved for a group—as if he had, in himself, constituted the third tribunal of which I speak. "Father, forgive them, for they know not what they do."

Recalling the events of our own lives, and those of earlier times, we cannot help but be struck by the monotonous repetition of violent crimes: we make war, spill blood, wound and kill innocents, children and women, exploit the weak and the poor, impose vain hierarchies, inflict physical cruelty, sexual and emotional humiliation, delight every day in the spectacle of death. We ought at least to have learned by now what we do, and what our ancestors have done since the beginning of human time. How can we be unaware of this original sin, this murderous impulse, written down, in all its darkness, in our souls and continually in our history? Only a God of infinite mercy could forgive us this infinite series of infamous deeds and the thoughtlessness with which we ceaselessly repeat them.

Recall once again the words of Christ, beseeching God to erase the abominable record of chronic human misconduct: "Father, forgive *them*, for *they* know not what *they* do." Who is this "them," who is this "they"? They are the members of the human race. Christ died in order to wash away the sins of the world—the sins of all people. Of humanity.

The Gospel account of the Passion turns our ideas of judgment upside down. When Christ said, "My kingdom is not of this world" (John 18:36), he challenged our common understanding of lawfulness. It is not only the Sanhedrin, which pronounced an unjust sentence, or the small group that warmed itself next to the fire, but virtually all the tribunals known to history, and our deadly passion to find culprits, that are called into question by the account of the Passion. A rare reversal of perspective.

Saint Peter's Tears and the Casting of the First Stone
Disconsolate at having denied his master, Peter wept. We, too, weep bitter tears over our many failings and transgressions. We do not cease to grieve at what we have done, to mourn our unworthiness.

After his disciple had shed these tears, Jesus Christ died in order to wash away the sins of the world. What does this word mean, the "world"? All of us, certainly, which is to say each of us, taken separately, individually; but also, and above all, all of us, taken together.

Not only with Peter, but also with the Prophets, and with Jesus Christ himself, I mourn collective sins, those of the particular tribunal that sentenced the Innocent to the torments of the cross as well as those of humanity in general, for whom the Innocent gave his life on Good Friday.

Peter wept. It is through the gift of tears that saints are recognized. Saint Peter wept.

Let us reread the account of the woman charged with adultery: "As they continued to ask him, [Jesus] stood up and said to them, "Let him who is without sin among you be the first to throw a stone at her" (John 8:7). The first objection to the iniquity of this stoning has to do with the asymmetry of the punishment. Evidently the woman who was caught unawares did not consummate the act all alone;

the group, owing to its immemorial hatred of women, ex-
cused her companion. When Jesus began to write on the
ground with his finger, did he spell out—and, if so, did he
show or did he conceal—the name of the one who seduced
her and who now abandoned her? And when he called upon
a man without sin to come forward, did he apostrophize the
one whose name could be deciphered on the ground? Was
this the oldest one among them, the one who was the first
to step back? His identity hardly matters, there was at least
one such person.

What matters to me is the "at least one." For I know
him. Not by name, but by his presence and his function—I
was about to say, his usefulness. In a firing squad, he is the
one whose rifle, issued at random, is loaded with a blank
cartridge. Why is this blank necessary? Why is it necessary
that, among the executioners, this "at least one" does not
kill? Why should he be chosen, in effect, by drawing lots?
For the same reason, a profound one. For in the wake of a
death by stoning or by shooting, judicial review—or a palace revolt, or a popular revolution—may bring to light the
innocence of the person who was executed. In that event
the situation is reversed, and the people will turn on those
who killed the now blameless defendant, which is to say the
entire firing squad. But who among this group really killed
the one who in the meantime has become a victim? In the
case of the biblical stoning, responsibility is clear: struck in
the temple, the woman crumbled to the ground, dead. You,
you killed her, we saw you cast the first stone. But among
those who fire with a rifle, the one who drew the blank cartridge can claim that he did not kill; he is therefore relieved
of all responsibility. Because his rifle was issued at random,
no one knows which rifle contained the blank, and so each

member of the firing squad can plausibly claim that the rifle was his; accordingly, no member of the firing squad bears responsibility for the death. Since each member may be presumed innocent, the firing squad itself bears responsibility. Here, however, responsibility is hidden—in this case by the luck of the draw.

Regression to the Infinite and Its Empty Limit

Otherwise an endless regression is entailed: the one who casts the first stone, hitting the victim in the head and killing her on the first try, bears responsibility for her death; this person then becomes the excuse for a second execution, by way of reprisal. The killer becomes a victim in his turn. This process is repeated for as long as it takes until finally the entire group of witnesses is killed off. The worldwide success of Agatha Christie's *And Then There Were None* derived from the same terrifying dynamic. The Gospel text is meant to warn against just this danger of collective extinction—the asymptotic destiny of all violence, on a larger scale. Violence, and the vengeance it automatically provokes, sets in motion an infinite sequence whose limit empties the earth of human beings.

From the Christian point of view, a sacrificial lynching, far from resolving social conflict, as pagan mythology assumes, threatens ultimately to kill off human society altogether. It is therefore necessary to put an end to violence, once and for all. And this by beginning with the one who cast the first stone, the one who is truly responsible, and perhaps twice over; no doubt he was the first to rush forward to see that the woman was dead, because he had sinned with her. Now there was no one to testify against him.

Here, then, we have a quasi-arithmetic of sacrifice, and of the mortal risk, under cover of self-preservation, that violence forces society to incur. It has nothing to do with sociology, or the anthropology of violence, or even law. It has to do with the final horizon of violence, what it leads to in the end.

The Gospel text has a Jewish antecedent, the tenth chapter of the Talmud, known as Tractate Sanhedrin, which authorizes witnesses, and only witnesses, to throw the first stones at those whom their testimony has sentenced to death. In the event that one day the high court's ruling is overturned on appeal, the witnesses will be held responsible for the court's error, and the cycle of retribution will start up all over again. Jesus altered the traditional legal arrangement in a subtle but crucial way, by inviting to come forward, not witnesses, but one who was impeccable, in the root sense of the word—incapable of sinning. Witnesses there very well might be, of course; but did such a person as the one Jesus summoned actually exist, one who had never sinned, one who had not once failed to observe *the whole Law*?

Ceremonial Rereadings

Following Peter's crucifixion, following the execution of the adulterous woman, there were funeral ceremonies. Burying a cadaver: a sacred act, another spectacle, a new relation to death. Trials and obsequies, ritual activities both, attract crowds by binding people together, tragically. *Religion* does not cease working.

Many of the stories I have recalled so far unfolded in a city, Jerusalem in particular. Whereas the countryside disperses, the city brings together. Let us therefore remain in the city. What relation does it have to death? The boulevards that encircle Paris, just inside the city limits, bear the names

of Napoleon's twelve marshals, high-ranking officers who pre-
sided over campaigns in which tens of thousands of soldiers
died, victims all. The account of history I give in my book
Rome: Le Livre des fondations (1983) records similar numbers,
naming the names of killers who have been celebrated as
heroes; a true philosophy of history, to my way of thinking,
therefore consists in putting itself in the place of the victims.

For a great many years I did not attend a public ceremony in
which soldiers passed by, marching in close formation. Nowa-
days burials are rarely followed by ceremonial processions,
and since in any case the boredom of official occasions keeps
crowds away, fewer people attend them than in the past.

Not quite two decades ago, in 2001, the Académie française paid a final tribute to Léopold Sédar Senghor, who
had died in Normandy and was subsequently buried in
Dakar. Following my election to the Académie in 1990 we
talked together often; I was very fond of him, we became
close. After his passing, in the nave of the church of Saint-
Germain-des-Prés in Paris, a cardinal officiated before the
president of France and the prime minister, accompanied by
their wives, the four of them seated behind the balustrade
of the choir.

Senghor, a Christian, a graduate of the École Normale
Supérieure, and a Latinist, had asked that the Mass be celebrated with Gregorian chant; traditional Wolof songs and
the drumming of the village where he was born evoked his
Senegalese heritage. Academic, poet, statesman—did his de-
parted soul hear the dark eloquence that filled the sanctuary,
in keeping with his wishes?

The church was full, the sidewalks outside overflowing
with curious bystanders.

In the Village of Carere

Catholic ceremonies often incorporate certain rites taken over from ancient Rome, together with Jewish liturgies. Here the Euro-African space, rebuilt in music, was nestled inside a pocket of time that Senghor himself had sewn, by claiming—rightly or wrongly, I cannot say—that plainsong came from the recitatives of negritude. For neither white Rome, nor mixed-race Christianity, nor black Africa, nor the prophetic writers of ancient Israel can boast of having invented the word "ceremony." Of Etruscan origin (according to our classical sources, the city of Carere gave it its name)—an origin concealed by the Latin armies that eliminated a people whose genius taught the Mediterranean world the delicacy of art, an original approach to death, and a certain conception of piety that was to make a lasting impression on the minds of neighboring peoples—ceremonies were adopted everywhere without anyone remembering who were the first ones to practice them. What lost meaning does this intertemporal music express, from what dark and unknown tomb does this music rush forth?

Spectacle

The mourners were gathered together in remembrance of the deceased. There, in the church of Saint-Germain-des-Prés, all of them were confronted with a phantom. Three questions. First, did they kneel before the God in whom Senghor believed, praying to Him, all of them, in his presence? Did this unique and dual absence unite them? Or, second, to the contrary, did it split them into two groups, with the majority casting sidelong glances at the petty masters of the moment? Outside, dumbfounded, the passersby had gawked at the president and the prime minister as they went into the church, at the black chasubles, and at the green coats of the members of the Académie française. Or, third, was the assembly divided instead into three, with the decorated writers and notables inside making up a middle group that sought to be admired by the little people outside, who saw them raised up in the company of the great?

In the first case, transcendence ensures the cohesiveness of a group of designated mourners. In the second, mutual regard produces social cohesiveness in its own way, to one degree or another, as all such ceremonies are meant to do. The third case, more dynamically, calls attention to the longing for social advancement: the masses are encouraged in the belief that democracy provides them with the opportunity, if fortune smiles, of becoming famous themselves.

In all these cases, some one (or ones), absent or present, unique, rare, or common, turns around to face the congregation. These changes in orientation are revelatory. The officiant prays, his face turned toward us. The reader gets up from his seat, mounts the podium, and reads the Gospel text that we listen to. The Perpetual Secretary of the Academy, followed by the President of the Republic, speaks before all of us in memory of the deceased. We know these leaders, often we give them a name; only transcendence, which is unnamable, fails to show its face. In confronting these authorities, turned around to confront us in their turn, we live together. A group of equals, face-to-face; face-to-face, an equal bond.

The religious rite—representation, memorial, theater—thus meets up with the spectacle of social and religious power. Can it be reduced to this spectacle?

A Unique Ceremony

Funeral services may be traced back to the earliest human cultures; ethnologists and anthropologists have found evidence of them at all latitudes, in the vicinity of power and not far from death. Recently, however, under the influence of technology, they have undergone an extraordinary change, in defiance of archaic religious prohibitions and protocols. Now, a handful of people whose faces no one notices, though they too are turned toward us, carry headphones, cameras, high-fidelity microphones, and booms on their shoulders, in their hands, and on their heads, in a dazzling light that floods the sanctuary, trailing cables in loops and braids that high-ranking officials, like everyone else, are apt to trip over. Tomorrow, on television screens throughout a region, or a nation, or the entire world, depending on the importance of the ceremony, ten thousand or millions will attend the same rite, retransmitted in bits and pieces. Not only do people of moderate notoriety therefore have less interest than they once did in making themselves seen in person by the anony-mous, gathered outside in relatively small numbers on the street, but even the most eminent figures themselves hasten to make themselves seen from the neck up in the lens of these cameras, which, facing all of us, will arrange matters so that everyone, great, medium, and small, henceforth will exist together only for, before, and through them. For these cameras have seized hold of social ties, manufacturing them in their turn; they alone now bind people together.

The ceremony—Roman, Christian, African, Etruscan; ar-chaic, efficacious for that very reason, ultimately forgotten— now draws to a close, after only a relatively brief existence, owing to a loss of function and utility. What need is there for eloquence, for mighty organs and choirs shrouded in dark mysteries, when the technicians who will edit the camera footage can be counted on to delete the plainsong,

Couperin's music, the tom-toms and the Wolof songs (too long), the most sublime beauties of the service itself (too profound), the vaults and pillars (too large and too high), in order to show, in the space of a minute, the uncertain steps of elderly grandees coming out of the church, elbowing their way forward in order to flaunt themselves, not before the bystanders massed beneath the portico, who no longer count for much, but before an aperture that, this evening or tomorrow, will unite a far larger audience, virtual and invisible, the only social reality that still coheres today?

Whom shall we now call great if not the editor who is prepared to cut off the feet and legs and, if need be, the torsos of the assembled eminences, so that their images will fit on the screen? Farewell to Etruria, farewell to numberless ancient rites; the only ceremony there is today plays out before an array of audiovisual recording devices. In the modern sanctuary, the real officiants wear neither chasuble nor green coat nor tricolor sash; with arms extended, they hold cameras and lighting booms. These are the new priests.

Glory

By means of these devices, the image replaces corporeal presence. This transition to the virtual reveals part of the secret. But we need to keep in mind that the ceremony itself has always produced this same virtual reality; the Etruscans had no doubt invented it with this purpose in mind, so that it would fill the political space between multiplicity and unicity. Ancient ceremonies were already transitions to the image, at least through a virtual and gentle exchange of glances.

This exchange of glances—televised images, in their modern incarnation—holds human beings together through the spectacle of glory, which is to say glory itself. Whether it unites or divides the spectators, they remain bound together by the immanent cohesion of society; if, by contrast, glory is given to God alone, transcendence, by this gift, binds believers together. Informative, symbolic, and virtual—in a word, negentropic—this immanent, gentle, vainglorious cohesiveness comes back, on our screens, from the virtual to a sort of reality by giving substance to the exchanged glances of society. It may also, in becoming actual, one day be transubstantiated into hard forces on the entropic scale, devastating in their effects, destroying lives and cities; for the time being, however, it remains potential, innocuous, inoffensive. Yet in the case of funerals, and in the media, it presupposes and conceals death.

What is new is that the images on our screens, whether real or virtual, depend on the reduction of all glances to a single one, the one recorded by the camera, and its retransmission via electronic devices. Thus the gentleness of mutual glances is converted by a hard machine into soft messages—the same dual transubstantiation we observe in those webs of relations that are rightly called social networks.

We have now manufactured a machine, in other words, for manufacturing gods. False gods?

Machines

We have now succeeded in designing and constructing tools, out of glass and plastic materials, all quite real, that are capable of realizing a virtual world of exchanged glances; networked machines that suck up, store, and distribute images, to be sure, but that also, by means of them, spread the immanent, gentle, vainglorious cohesiveness I mentioned a moment ago. It dazzles us with the light that the cameramen shined inside the church of Saint-Germain-des-Prés, facing us, in the choir. Their machines transubstantiated a ceremony witnessed by three hundred persons into one witnessed by millions; they have the immense and novel power to change the scale of events, and therefore to transform virtual powers into gigantic potentials. Someone who is already powerful, who is seen in them and acts through them, can seduce the world and set it ablaze.

There is now only one ceremony, the one that is produced by these machines, which, in extending their reach everywhere, have replaced all other ceremonies. There is now only one officiant in the choir: the aperture, or lens, which in French is called *l'objectif*, ironically, since it has only subjective and collective functions. This is why, once again, we miss other occasions; we now attend only one ceremony, which takes place every day. There is now only one rite and one Church: the Media—aptly named, since it has replaced the Meditator of John 14:6. We begin to suspect that the machine for manufacturing gods functions in a closed circuit, that the operators of this machine realize that they themselves have become gods . . . False gods?

Residual Religion

In memory of Léopold Sédar Senghor and of his faith, believers gathered together in the sanctuary, confronted by the mystery of the Eucharist. There stood the priests, facing us, bent over this transcendent transubstantiation, their eyes closed. In the same sanctuary and at the same time, cameras reproduced an immanent transubstantiation for a mass audience, flooding us with light.

Are we changing religion? There is now only one, the relation constituted by the various mass media; this new religion, universal and permanent, has obliterated the efficacy of all others. It has now obtained for itself a monopoly. At noon and in the evening we turn on the television news and make our prayer to the anchor, who appears in a studio of wood and glass, a sort of cross between fetish and idol, facing the audience, virtually assembled. This is surely a ceremony, indeed a religious one. The cardinal and the officiants at Saint-Germain-des-Prés testified to the virtual absence of God; the television cameramen testified to the virtual absence of everyone else. These two priests, officiants and cameramen, by their presence, represent the absence of two almighty gods, the one transparent, the other immanent—the one true, the other false?

These two priests, standing in the same choir—are they opposed to one another? Must we choose between the absent transcendence to which all glory is granted, *Gloria in excelsis Deo*, and the growling, the snarling of a world devoted to competition, sometimes violent, a world determined to fabricate glory, to acquire it, keep it, perpetuate it? Must we bow down before the merciful all-weakness of the former or before the latter, our own merciless all-powerfulness? Weakness of the true, power of the false?

Or rather: since the two priests are distinguished corporeally, before our eyes, in the sanctuary and by the objects that they manipulate, we can no longer confuse social religion with a faith in God. Replacing the Mediator, the media have seized hold of *all* religion, insofar as it expresses a relation, and drained it of its power, leaving only one religion, independent of the ones that came before. At last a great day dawns: since no one fools us, we can no longer fool ourselves.

Here the camera, there the Eucharist; sociologists on the one hand, religious persons on the other. *False gods produce*

*the collective relations that produce false gods, but in the end
serve as filters of the truth.*

Other Funeral Ceremonies

How are these false gods manufactured? We have witnessed
similar ceremonies, when Lady Diana died, for example, or
the French pop star Johnny Hallyday, collective observances
in which one encounters once more what the Romans called
apotheosis, which is to say deification. We saw then, still more
clearly than we did just a moment ago, the crowd transform
such people into gods.

Once again only a restricted group of family and close
friends had the privilege of entering the church where the
"true" ceremony took place. But these pseudo-faithful represented only a small fraction of all the stars, all the princes
and princesses in the world, themselves candidates for deification one day, without any attention being given to what
was going on in the choir, which no one cared about. The
consequences were the same as at Saint-Germain-des-Prés:
the assembly, apparently divided in two—the crowd milling
about outside on the sidewalks, the privileged few inside
the church—was actually divided into three, since thousands
of spectators, absent from the streets and from the temple,
followed the spectacle on their screens and via their social
networks, remotely sharing in the experience of those who
were actually present; all of them therefore were united by
these machines, except, of course, the faithful, whose prayers
escaped the flood of images. The vast socio-media machine,
producer of apotheosis, busy fashioning an idol, thrust aside
the God of monotheism, as though he were almost nothing. In the old church, the officiants prayed alone, ruthlessly
swept away by the pagan tsunami. When the machine for

manufacturing gods is operating at full capacity in the vicinity of this monotheism, the powerlessness of the old religion to recruit new followers is obvious. The communion of saints does not depend on a mass movement that creates its own foundation.

We have therefore witnessed a third kind of ceremony, this one quite unexpected, which acts as a filter whose gigantic sieve makes it possible to distinguish religion, pure and simple, from the social construction of gods; the religion, in other words, of those who are genuinely bound together. What a stroke of luck! We can now understand how the false—powerful, immense, intense, so facile and probable that it unfailingly produces collective agreement, but little information—comes to be separated from the true—subtle, fine, difficult to grasp, improbable, indeed exceedingly rare, but saturated with information.

Analysis and Synthesis
The blending, or synthesis, of several "religions" in these three cases permits a close analysis to be made that will reveal more clearly the world that sociologists try unsuccessfully to explain. We do not collectively produce the God of monotheism, he produces us; we do, however, produce the gods of polytheism, mechanically, as Bergson understood. This we know to be true, we have seen it at last with our own eyes. This is also why, in my view, polytheism can be considered the "natural" religion of every society; societies ceaselessly fabricate gods, sculpted from politics, sports, theater, music, the media. We produce them in producing the "we"; we produce the "we" in producing them. In earlier works I have called these gods "quasi-objects." Our tradition, lucidly, calls them "false gods."

So lucidly, in fact, that I wonder whether the distinction between the false and the true does not in fact derive from the filter I just mentioned. History relates the fight to the death of the Hebrew prophets against the kings, of the physicists against the Greek city-state, of research against consensus, of a solitary figure against the many, of inventors against experts, of the subtle against the obvious. In this contest, innovators lose every time. Truth becomes evident only once it has been adopted by the group as a whole, which makes a dogma of it, a received idea—at which point the battle starts all over again. Consensus has nothing to do with truth; many people in the past have given their lives to establish this obvious fact. Alas, in extending the power of the many, the media have placed the heritage of the ancient geometers and modern luminaries in grave crisis.

Epistemology of the False

From the Enlightenment onward, gradually but in the end completely, and quite rightly so, the mathematical and experimental sciences have taken away from religion, in this case Christianity, the prerogative of accounting for the genesis of the stars, the earth, the climate, and living creatures. Celestial mechanics and the other branches of astronomy, physics, chemistry, biology, and geology have deprived it of the power to explain the world. Associated with these sciences, including medicine, were instruments, methods, and remedies that proved to be more effective than the explanations (occasionally supplemented by miracles) devised by religious traditions. From the triumph of science, which was thought to have delivered a death blow to these traditions, there nonetheless followed a certain advantage from the theological point of view. Exegetes who persisted in their devotion to the letter of sacred texts lost their time, their credibility, and ultimately their line of work; others, no longer disturbed by scientific rationality, whose implications they were now free to investigate in their spare time, went on praying to God as before.

A second challenge came from the human sciences, softer in their way, which reduced religion and its ritual apparatus to collective human activities. The gods provided the foundation for civic life, united groups, produced social harmony; social harmony created the gods, the gods created social harmony. This change of perspective proved to be still more devastating than the first. It needs to be kept in mind that the new information machines, having in the meantime acquired a social purpose, stand in the same relation to the social sciences as tools functioning on the entropic scale do to the physical sciences. Thus the digital media, television, social networks, screens of all types, have come to monopolize ceremonies of every kind, which in the old polytheism likewise served to trap and ensnare crowds. Facing the gaze of the television news anchor, who is both absent and present, the virtual union of all came into being. Everything that proceeded from society or that preceded it, represented it, actualized it, heated it, transformed it, even studied it—sports, theater, cinema, books, education, legal proceedings, political assemblies, gatherings of all sorts, wars, scandals, assassinations—from now on occurs as spectacle, indeed exists only as spectacle and is recycled as spectacle, which transubstantiates a sparse crowd into a unity or totality. Spectacle appropriates everything that touches all of us, not least the compulsion to act in front of an audience, which for many people today amounts to existence itself, and which for almost all people is equivalent to the truth (one thinks of the ancient Greek concept of truth, *alétheia*, formulated in an age when consensus had not yet encountered the decisive novelty of demonstration). Nothing exists, socially speaking, without spectacle, which reflects social opinion only to the extent it has created it in the first place; the less it shapes society, the less society sees itself in it. Spectacle has become all but identical with society. Because society now has only a virtual existence for the most part, only being actualized from time to time through violence, wars, and other such means, machines for manufacturing virtuality are increasingly able to fashion every aspect of it.

All the preceding stories, of judgments, executions, and burials, took place in a city, Paris or Jerusalem. Let us now look down on the world from a greater height. Cities unite, the countryside disperses. Humanity, the largest social group of all, is divided into city dwellers and people who live in the country.

Epistles and Parables

> Phaedrus: You, my excellent friend, strike me as the oddest of men. Anyone would take you, as you say, for a stranger being shown the country by a guide, not for a native— never leaving the city to cross the frontier nor even, I believe, so much as setting foot outside its walls.
>
> Socrates: Forgive me, my dear friend. You see, I'm a lover of learning, and trees and open country won't teach me anything, whereas people in the city do.
>
>   Plato, Phaedrus 230c–d

Does one speak of "the Father's house" (John 14:2) in order to avoid having to say that the Son had no house? The four Gospels seldom use this word in connection with the Son of Man. The night of the agony, in the garden of Gethsemane, the apostles slept, wrapped in their cloaks; while their master moaned and despaired, they snored outside. After Jesus's transfiguration, Peter had offered to make three tabernacles, for him, Moses, and Elijah. After Jesus's crucifixion, the Roman soldiers drew lots for his garments, his only lodging.

Where, during the three years of his public life, did Jesus and the twelve disciples live? As far as one can tell, nowhere. They camped and, at night, slept in their cloaks. Thirteen homeless people, without even a stone to rest their head upon. We are told that Jesus knocked on the doors of a few people he knew, Lazarus and Zacharias, for example; he sat, barelegged, in the house of Martha and Mary Magdalene; the thirteen celebrated Passover in the house of friends, where the Last Supper took place and the washing of feet, the dusty feet of vagabonds. When Jesus spoke of work, he mentioned weaving, harvesting, sowing; building, only once or twice. He compared the plumage of birds to the royal robes of Solomon, who nonetheless was the great builder of Jewish tradition. Jesus neither dwelled in a house nor built anything; he was not even to occupy his own tomb for very long. Peter, well named, was later to build. And reign over the City.

The Countryside . . .

> Murs, ville,
> Et port,
> Asile
> De Mort . . .
> Victor Hugo, *Les Djinns*

Literally, and unmusically: Walls, city / And haven / Refuge / Of Death . . . Life: sower, mustard seed, lilies of the field, birds of the sky, straw, mote and beam, vine stock and shoots, harvest workers . . .—the parables related in the Gospels are steeped in rural culture; they are spoken on the banks of the River Jordan, in the desert, next to a lake, in the middle of a storm, in the company of fishermen; so, too, the famous Sermon on the Mount was preached *outdoors*. No house, no city, no politics: on the one side, God; on the other, Caesar. From these parables and the everyday circumstances of Christ's life there emanates a delicious fragrance, light, airy, bucolic, almost miraculous, that did not escape the notice, in his *Vie de Jésus*, of Ernest Renan, born in the French town of Tréguier—a fragrance familiar to anyone who has loved the outdoors, the land and the sea, anyone who has lived and worked there. But what could Renan learn from such a small rural town? What could Jesus of Nazareth learn from so small a village?

When Jesus entered Jerusalem, mounted on an ass, he trod on palm branches. He came to the city only to be judged and sentenced there, to suffer and die.

. . . *and the City*

Saint Paul, born in Tarsus, son of a Roman citizen, traveled from town to town, unlike his master, who nonetheless appeared to him on a road, *outside*. His Epistles were addressed to Corinthians, Colossians, Thessalonians, and Romans, among other city dwellers. Paul—and after him, Peter—urbanized a message that was rustic in its origins. The idea, widespread among historians and sociologists, that the Christian religion was founded, not by Christ, but by Paul, the apostle to the Gentiles, derives from a view of the world and of history according to which everything must come from cities and those who live in them, and that the people of the countryside are entitled only to silence. Jesus broke with this; the good news he brought had no urban affiliation. Its novelty—radiant, transparent, extrahistorical—was rural in its origins, just as Moses's message sprang from the river, from the mountain, from the desert sands: spaces that have no place in history. The evangelical light, gentle and pure, emerges from a noiseless expanse where there are neither walls nor streets. But who can hear a gospel spoken outside walls?

Four centuries after Saint Paul, Saint Augustine wrote *The City of God*, in which the opposition between, and the passage from, immanence to transcendence displays the symmetry and the antithesis of two cities. The Christian religion, having its seat in Rome, thus takes its name from the Eternal City. In order to enter into history, Roman Catholicism had to enter into a metropolis, and there into political life. In the present day, when megalopolises devour space and kill people who live outside them, can we find a place where we can listen to a message sent from a rustic village and its hinterland?

The ongoing destruction of our planet cannot be attributed to political decisions alone. Economic policies share responsibility for this state of affairs. We conceive of the economy, in order to characterize its operation and to forecast its future course, as an equilibrium among numberless transactions. Political life remains in cities, where we live among ourselves; confining our attention to the workings of the market, we conceive of the economy as if there were no wider world. City and market; not land, nor sea, nor mine.

History and Silence

As late as the nineteenth century only a small part of humanity inhabited cities, probably less than ten percent. It seems
reasonable to suppose that, going back in time, this number
continues to fall. And yet history reminds us of Ur in Chal-
dea, of Babylon and Jerusalem, Memphis and Alexandria,
Sparta and Athens, Rome and Carthage, Paris, Berlin and
Oxford, London and New York, Delhi and Tokyo—all urban
centers occupied by a minority of human beings, monopolists
of wealth and glory, fed by the people of the countryside,
mute for their part, parasitized, the foster fathers of humanity. History despises them, even though, since the Neolithic
and until very recently, the great majority of *Homo sapiens*
worked the land and lived on farms, planting crops and herd-
ing animals. I have often thought of writing a history of this
death struggle between city and countryside, steadily being
lost by the rural population, now on the verge of extinction.
Red alert: once there are no more farmers, what will we eat
next? Our own? Our walls?

Two Heretics of the Fields

It is only with Saint Francis of Assisi and the legends that
grew up around him—more than a thousand years after
Jesus—that we come back to the countryside, to the forest
of wolves, the sky of birds, and the fields of the *Fioretti*.
Poet and troubadour, suspected of paganism, Saint Francis
had the same attitude of wary submission and stubborn
opposition toward Rome that Jesus had toward Jerusalem,
the same attitude toward organized religion, urbanized,
politicized, ignorant of all mysticism. A wandering beggar,
il Poverello as he was known, he left his home and his place
of birth, barefooted; he lived on the roads and died in a

hut of cut branches, singing a canticle to the sun and to his fellow plants and beasts—to the *Biogea*, the name that I give to the Earth. He revived at long last the memory of the homeless Christ and prefigured, from a great distance, our secular sciences of earth and life, geology and biology. From Assisi and its environs there emanated the same fragrance of mystic lightness as the one that in Christ's time spread throughout Galilee. Jesus and Francis, unlike the city dwellers Paul and Augustine, were rural heretics. It would be better to call the one, not Jesus of Nazareth, but Jesus *outside of* Nazareth, and the other, not Francis of Assisi, but Francis *outside of* Assisi; both lived outside the walls of the small towns where they were born and spoke for the humble in the root sense of the Latin word *humus*: the Incarnation sprang from the soil, that is, from clay and humus, decomposed plant matter.

Country dwellers did not enjoy a title equivalent to that of citizen. So long as only a minority of human beings inhabited cities, almost all humanity could hear the Gospels. The countryside having in the meantime become mostly uninhabited, who now will hear it?

Envoi

This is why I sing of the flowers of the fields and of rural parables. Francis, his wolf, his birds, his *Fioretti*, composed in the chapel of the Porziuncola, far from the city, even from the City of God; La Fontaine, his *Fables*, in which wolf and lamb dispute amidst waters and forests, oak and reed; Michelet, lover of witches, who then turned his attention to nature in *The Sea, The Bird, The Mountain, The Insect*— all of these thinkers carried on the endangered tradition of the fields.

Since my beginnings in this free discipline, philosophy, I have lived in their landscape more often than in the political obsolescence of cities. Long ago, *sotto voce*, my book *Détachement* (1983) sang of the country dweller, the sailor, the wanderer, the Franciscan, the tree of life. Since then, in *Nouvelles du monde* (1996), *Paysages des sciences* (1999), *Rameaux* (2007), *Biogée* (2010), and *Le Contrat naturel* (2018) I have tried to deepen this line of inquiry.

Anyone who has never left the city, where everything, streets, walls, and institutions, has been constructed by human hands, believes that only our works exist, that nothing exists outside of us. The peasant, the sailor, learn the hard way that they always find in front of them, around them, and sometimes against them a world that encompasses and goes beyond them, that at every moment and under every circumstance is stronger than they are; living and working in something that is other than human, they do not have the same relationship to politics and history as city dwellers. For those who live in cities, man is God; for those who live in the countryside, God, if he exists, is not man. City dwellers begot Marx; sailors and their country cousins fraternize with Spinoza. The human sciences inhabit cities; the hard sciences wander outside their walls.

As against Socrates in the *Phaedrus*, people in the city teach me nothing; the countryside and its trees, they teach me everything. Nothing means only that which is human, everything means nature, the very stream in which humanity bathes. If I believe, I believe *in* God. *Deus sive natura.*

Let us distinguish between two types of existence, two types of human being. Living outside, exposed to the elements, country folk and sailors are never able to cast off their condition, of being-in-the-world. Jesus, for his part, spoke of the sower and walked on the lake, homeless. The offspring of city dwellers, raised within the four walls of an apartment and the two cliffs of a street, find their mental horizons reduced to family relations and, seduced by the charms of psycho-analysis, readily find their way from this cramped world to the depths of conscience; recall Oedipus, king of Thebes, the presumptive killer of his father and lover of his mother. Surrounded by overpowering things that do not depend on them, left with no alternative but a synthesis between these things and the ones that submit to their works and deeds, country folk and sailors are intimately familiar with the bonds that lastingly link heaven and earth with the violence that sometimes, however rarely, unites the dispersed creatures of this wide world. Here, then, we have two ways, external and internal, each one a stranger to the other, of being bound together. Two ways of experiencing and conceiving of the religious impulse?

The Conflict between City and Country

The rusticity of the Gospels makes us aware of Jesus's ha-tred of urban religion, of the Pharisees and the merchants and the moneychangers of the Temple—a wrath that I have called heretical. Jesus deeply mistrusted the tawdry theater that civil society cannot do without. This feeling inspired loyalty, toward himself and toward the apostles; more than this, it instilled in his followers a mystic conception of re-ligion. Péguy was not the first to point out the distinction between the mystical and the political; it is patent in the Gospels themselves.

Mysticism, true religion. False gods founded cities; they were raised up in the course of funeral ceremonies, court proceedings, and executions, gatherings and assemblies of all kinds—as a consequence of politics, in general, inasmuch as this term designates the city itself. There, in the city, everything is political—indeed, the two words derive from the same Greek root; outside the city, there is something that goes beyond our individual works and destinies. *Natura sive Deus.*

Merciful Paganism

Nevertheless let us not forget that both peasant and pagan had a similar feeling about nature, and even gave it a name. One thing I especially like about Catholicism, the heir in this respect of the rustic Gospels, is the anthropological wisdom of blending monotheism with a worship of saints, relatives of the false gods of polytheism; monotheism has sometimes even borrowed from polytheism. What is a martyr if not an innocent victim, a false god not unlike a true one? This earthly, realistic—I was about to say anthropological—clemency, this wide-ranging and supple synthesis, close to the people, coal miners and old women, permits it to avoid the abstract, exclusionary, sometimes violent radicalism found in certain strict monotheisms. Saint Francis, a rural mystic, guarded against the Inquisition.

I remember, as a child, having assisted the priest during the observance of Rogation Days, days of prayer and fasting before the Feast of the Ascension. On leaving the village, under Aquitaine's pastel skies, followed, in procession, by the local farmers and artisans, the priest, a man of the country, blessed the *pagus*: sprouting wheat, green vines, pasturelands and wetlands. A man of the country, which is to say still a pagan, and an environmentalist before his time. Did his aspergillum write down in that immanent rural space, haunted by dryads and naiads, a first draft of my *Biogée*? No, he followed in the steps of Christ, amidst the springtime in Quercy, as gentle as the springtime in Galilee and Umbria, amidst the clip-clop chant of horseshoes, among the barely opened buds of the cherry trees. As pagans and/or Christians, do we therefore pray both to the true God and to wood nymphs? To the pagan gods, assuredly. Would we know the difference?

From the Land to the City

Perhaps we should know the difference, because the modern West benefited from a unique circumstance. Little by little, then en masse, it converted to an imported religion, born on another land than ours, the Holy Land, in Palestine, where the sacred story unfolded, the story of the Hebrew people and that of the Redemption to come, whose coming is guaranteed. The decisive events for our salvation took place elsewhere; they involve figures other than the ones we know from our own local histories. Neither geography nor history—each of them holy—unfolded beneath our feet.

By not sacralizing their own soil, the peoples of the West came to separate the spiritual from their chthonic roots and abandoned the *pagus* of paganism. The West was deterritorialized from the beginning; or rather, this abrupt bifurcation was a consequence of its having been deracinated, uprooted from the soil.

The sacred enterprise that began with the exodus of the Hebrew people to the promised land, and that then was taken to an extreme by the Christians, led them, the Christians, to consider this land of milk and honey to be inaccessible here below, on earth: exiled from it, we will never be able to go back; henceforth, we must hope and aspire to enter the heavenly Jerusalem. Modernity could not emerge so long as it was conceived without this abstraction from the soil of the immanent world, without Saint Augustine's distinction between the Earthly City and the City of God.

How many lives did this hope spare in times of war *pro aris et focis*, for altars and hearths, for the fatherland, sacred land of the elders, cruel and deadly stepmother? How many more would it save today?

Having thus clarified the crucial relation between city and country, between the pagan *pagus* of the false gods and the city of the sole true God, how are we to find our way from the ones to the Other, from politics to mysticism, from humans bound together, to one another, to what releases them from these bonds?

On Spiritual and Temporal Powers
Surveying the world and humanity from a still greater height, another way of binding human beings together reveals itself, one that once again comes under the head of religion. For a spiritual power can unite groups that temporal powers— political, economic, military—divide and pull apart. Thus Asiatic religions, Judaism, Islam, and Christianity jointly federalize the many nations of the world.

This is why Comte dreamed of a religion of all humanity, through a third type of integration. At a moment when the Worldwide Web puts us in contact with information and one another instantaneously, dissolving the distances of space and time; when smartphones allow each of us to hold the world in his hand, how can we not share Comte's dream today? How otherwise will we be able to escape the economic globalization that we are experiencing today, a worldwide integration of commerce and finance that, by means of new technologies, encompasses the whole of relations, linkages, and ways of binding us together? At the very moment when globalization begins actually to exist, humanity finds itself in the grips of false gods as novel as they are archaic, detectable in space and over time, fabulously rich, and ceaselessly concentrating our attention on the screens they dominate. By their absence, the spiritual and the transcendent alone give hope of being able to free ourselves from the hold of this power, a temporal power, to be sure, but global in its reach. The return to religious belief that we are witnessing today may be an expression of this hope.

What merciful god will save us from Hermes in his modern guise, the Four Horsemen (Google, Apple, Facebook, Amazon), now permanently installed in our homes, constantly surveilling us? I no longer look at Hermes as I used to; or rather, I now realize that Hermes looks at me, looks at all of us, always and everywhere. I search therefore for a way to liberate myself, liberate all of us, from this false god, at once virtual and real. There can be no doubt of its falseness, since we have made it with our own hands, and since its power nonetheless overwhelms us, robs us, and subjugates us. Never has our need for a true god, absent and transcendent, been so great. Never have we been so near to it, never have we been as far from it.

The tautological expression "temporal power" speaks twice of force, twice requires submission; the paradoxical expression "spiritual power" implies that the greater the degree of spirituality, the less any real power is exercised. From a more elevated perspective, then, we see that the spiritual—aerial, extensive, tending toward ubiquity—stands opposed to the temporal—intensive, hard, solid, and local. The one weak, therefore global; the other strong, but partial.

Mortal Hardness, Floral Softness

Religion, I repeat, binds together in two ways, vertically and horizontally. First, it joins heaven to earth, which sometimes preserves a physical record of past hot spots, imprinted on its surface. Second, it unites sects, groups, and indeed society, humanity as a whole. We have just examined this second aspect of religion from progressively higher vantage points, while also contemplating a series of spectacles associated with death, each one larger than the last, all of them tragic in nature, three tribunals and three funeral ceremonies.

No ancient city was without a temple and a circus, the first for sacrifices, the second for killing; no contemporary city is without a theater, where tragedies are often staged, or a stadium, sometimes a *plaza des toros*, where killing is done. In the countryside there is no temple, only the sky, invisible within the walls of cities. But the city kills off the countryside, brutalizing it with chemistry and media displays. How does the human, horizontal bond come to be established, given that it concerns the group less than individuals? Answer: through the Gospel, through love. How, then, does it emerge in history? I will tell you.

Three Sacrifices

The history of religions, or at least the ones descended from Abraham, is characterized by what may be called a law of three stages. In certain archaic ceremonies a human being was sacrificed, often a woman or a child. In the biblical book of Judges, Jephthah's daughter dies at the hands of her father. Victorious over the Ammonites, Jephthah had vowed, as the price of his good fortune, to sacrifice the first one to come out of the door of his house to meet him; in the event, it was his own daughter who came to meet him, dancing and singing in celebration of his triumph. Similarly, among the Greeks, Iphigenia, daughter of Agamemnon, dies at the hands of her father, commander of the troops en route to Troy, whose fleet, owing to the wrath of a goddess, was prevented from sailing for lack of a favorable breeze; Agamemnon, in other words, killed his own child for the sake of wind. The Aztecs, atop their pyramids, dismembered and flayed the victim, and the priest donned his skin.

First of the three stages: human sacrifice, a tragic spectacle unfolding before a crowd of fascinated soldiers and believers. What tribunal had decided to put the wretched victim to death? Let us never forget that people eagerly rushed forward, in large numbers, wild-eyed, to witness capital punishment; that still today deadly accidents attract thousands of onlookers; that, having learned this age-old lesson, our funereal media, in order to boost their ratings, announce and visually document catastrophes, violent attacks, and murders, covering society with a grim veil of pessimism and melancholy.

But we have also seen, beginning with a simple execution, the peril to which human sacrifice exposes us, of eradicating our own species.

A First Step Forward

The book of Genesis tells us of the first step that needed to be taken in order to abolish this abomination. Just as he was about to kill his son Isaac, Abraham turned away his knife and sacrificed instead a ram that was caught in a nearby thicket by its horns. Judaism, the first of the major Abrahamic religions (along with Christianity and Islam), was born with this shift from human sacrifice to animal sacrifice. Still today we venerate these three faiths, while lamenting the survival from time to time of archaic practices.

Bull running, an age-old tradition that has come down to the present day, chiefly in Spanish-speaking countries, occupies an unexpected place in this long story—unexpected because of its civilizing influence, which can be seen in historical perspective. The bullfight itself commemorates the solemn moment when our ancestors renounced human sacrifice; the violence embodied by the crowd that packs a round arena, chanting ¡*olé*! in a continuous loop, now falls instead upon a beast, domesticated long ago in order to be slaughtered. I am not the first to note that animal sacrifice is devoted exclusively to killing domesticated beasts, raised among us so that we may eat them.

The account involving Abraham and Isaac is a snapshot, capturing the precise moment, the tragic hesitation, the holy decision when the hand of the sacrificer is diverted from the son to the ram. Centuries later, in an arena filled with impassioned spectators, the corrida culminates in a series of passes, so subtle and seamless that only afficionados can appreciate them; until the end, no one knows who will die, the bull or the matador. Sometimes it is the matador. Manolete died from a horn wound in Linares, in August 1947, at five o'clock in the afternoon; others have died in other arenas, Joselito, Balderas, Paquirri, along with still others, less famous. But more often it is the bull that dies, having collapsed after being pierced by the symmetrically filed tip of a sword, hidden under the matador's cape and suddenly thrust between the animal's shoulder blades. In the discourse of the corrida, the matador's triumph is compared to the intervention of an angel—an unconscious recollection of the divine messenger who, according to the biblical account, caused the knife to be redirected from Isaac's neck to the throat of the horned ram.

The bullfight is essentially Abrahamic, then, because it recalls the moment when the object of religious sacrifice shifted from human beings to fauna. Many people consider bullfighting to be a savage ceremony. The reason for this, I believe, is that we have long been living in a floral age of sweetness and innocence, of bread and wine.

A parenthetical question. Have those who advocate a thoroughgoing vegetarianism and call for the abolition of bull running paused to consider what would happen in the event that their views were to prevail? All domesticated animals would disappear. Instead of killing them in slaughterhouses and arenas, they would be killed off as a species in one fell swoop. Evidently the remedy is worse than the evil.

Animal sacrifice represents a second stage in the evolution of religious belief, not yet ended. Still today our Muslim friends kill lambs, on the holiday of Eid al-Adha, a feast commemorating Abraham's sacrifice.

Echoes of Jonah

The New Testament, at Matthew 8:23–27, relates that Jesus was sleeping, on a boat, when a storm arose on the sea. The Old Testament, at Jonah 1:4–15, relates that Jonah was sleeping, in the hold of a ship, when a mighty tempest came over the sea.

Calmed at once by the words of a man, on the one hand, and by the sacrifice of a man, on the other, a terrible hurricane had aroused the fury of sailors, still greater than that of the waves. In each case, a crisis caused men to fight one another. The story of the great flood from which Noah saved himself contains within it another story, a war of all against all that ends up exterminating everyone, apart from a single survivor; in its vividness and detail, however, it is more realistic, truer to human nature, than the abstractions of Hobbes and Rousseau.

Jonah, in the Old Testament account, admits the error of his ways to the men of the ship: "For I know that it is because of me that this great tempest has come upon you." The sailors then threw him into the sea, and the storm ceased at once to rage. The sacrifice of a single person sufficed to pacify fierce passions and to restore goodwill among the ship's crew. Matthew, for his part, relates that Jesus "rose and rebuked the winds and the sea; and there was a great calm. And the men marveled, saying, 'What sort of man is this, that even winds and sea obey him?'"

The sailors who cast Jonah into the crashing waves could have asked themselves the same question but did not—so persuaded were they, like the victim himself, that one man, through his own waywardness, could provoke the fury of the waves, and that they could be stilled by his sacrifice. We moderns, knowing Jonah to have been innocent of the crime imputed to him, find the outcome in his case no less miraculous than in the case of Jesus; impossible, in fact, so far as the calming of turbulent seas is concerned, but not at all with regard to putting an end to collective violence. Jesus taught that words, in the form of threat and persuasion, can dispel hatreds and forestall quarrels. A peaceful solution.

A Decisive Transition

Pay close attention, this is important. The Book of Jonah passes from human sacrifice to the absence of sacrifice, since the sacrificed hero is saved from drowning—though *not without the aid of an animal*: just as the ram saves Isaac from death, the great fish vomits up Jonah onto dry land, having swallowed him and kept him in its belly for three days and three nights, as many as Jesus was later to spend in the tomb. In Genesis, in order to save the son, the ram dies. In Jonah, a further step forward is taken: neither the man nor the fish dies; like the ram earlier, *the animal saves the man, only here it does not die.*

In Jonah, in other words, human sacrifice has been dispensed with: the man is saved, as the child Isaac had been before; but now animal sacrifice is dispensed with as well, since the whale, in saving the man, does not perish. This marks a second step forward: the animal does not die.

Similarly, in Jerusalem, Jesus was later to drive the merchants out of the Temple. Greeks, Latins, and Hebrews had all transformed their places of worship into slaughterhouses, streaming with blood, where fowl, sheep, cattle, and pigs were put to death. At the entrance to these sanctuaries, the faithful could buy an animal of their choosing and have it bled. Jesus drove out the sellers of these creatures in order to abolish this practice.

From Fauna to Flora

How, then, was sacrifice to be wholly forgotten? Once again, by putting forward a vicariant—a substitute victim. The ram caught in the thicket took the place of Isaac, just as the bull in the ring takes the place of the matador. That is what is new.

Toward the end of the four Gospels there is a further echo of the swerve of Abraham's knife, only now *from fauna, from ram, whale, sheep, and bull, to flora, to bread and wine.* Uniting the Last Supper of Thursday night and the Passion of Friday with the Sunday of the Resurrection, the sacrifice of the Catholic Mass commemorates the sacred moment when the host and the wine drunk from the chalice are transformed into the flesh and blood of Christ. Is this spectacle, once again and as always, founded on the death of a victim?

Let us sum up. Thou shalt no longer kill a human being, only an animal: Old Testament. New Testament: no longer shalt thou kill man or animal, thou shalt consume bread and wine. Here the story of Jonah indicated the way forward, by establishing an equilibrium between the three stages, since there neither man nor animal dies; that the fish should have vomited up the victim onto dry land is proof of victory over death, not once but twice. In this account many commentators have detected a harbinger of the resurrection of Christ, whose body and blood are met with once more in the form of bread and wine.

On the Eucharist

Christian tradition and theology have not ceased to wonder about this transition from body and blood to bread and wine and, in its extreme form, the dogma of the Real Presence of Christ in the Eucharist, the miraculous metamorphosis of these substances, two by two. The enigma of this presence, subsequently obscured by Scholastic metaphysics, which spoke of a transubstantiation, is cleared up once the Eucharist is put back at the end of this story, an anthropological drama in three acts. The Eucharist brings it to a close through a short circuit between the blood-drenched sacrifice of a man—the Passion of Jesus Christ—and the manducation of foods derived from floral species, grape and wheat.

Does the Eucharist skip the first two stages of sacrifice, human and animal? Yes and no, for the Resurrection of the Sunday compensates for the death of the Friday; yes and no, for I do not know whether the twelve apostles, at the Last Supper, ate a Passover lamb, which had now suddenly become, not a scapegoat, but the lamb of God, the God who washes away the sins of the world—a mystic lamb, in other words. Neither man nor animal dies. These sacrifices form a historical loop: Christ, the man, is dead, but is brought back to life; the lamb, the animal, is sublimated. From fauna we arrive finally at flora, bread and wine. Thus the sacrifice of the Mass.

Between these three crucial moments, two bifurcations intervene. First, the solemn moment when Abraham's knife, raised, held aloft, hesitates and then swerves from his son toward the ram. Second, in its savage culmination, the bull-fight hesitates between the groin of the matador, clothed in light, and the horn of the bull, clothed in darkness; in the sacrament, the bread becomes the body and the body becomes the bread, the wine becomes the blood and the blood becomes the wine.

Abraham raises his knife atop a mountain; the matador dances in the middle of the arena; the killings of the altars send forth rivers of blood; Jesus drives out the merchants from the Temple; Jonah and Jesus calm the turbulent seas; finally, the Last Supper, so often represented in painting, repeated every day—all these tragic scenes, these tragic spectacles, are concerned with death; all of them are ways of bringing people together in large numbers, in crowds, of binding them together.

Finally, A Third Stage

Thou shalt no longer kill man or woman or child; thou shalt no longer strangle, thou shalt no longer bleed ram or bull; thou shalt eat bread and thou shalt drink wine. The sacrament

of Holy Communion, the Eucharist, announced the advent
of an age of innocence, undefiled by killing, gently floral.
Plants are autotrophic, whereas animals are heterotrophic:
the latter subsist at the expense of other living creatures; the
former depend for their existence only on material molecules,
on water, on sun and light, and survive independently of living creatures. Plants do not kill. Flesh and blood, the result
of ancient sacrifices, are both transformed into nonsacrificial
states, bread and wine.

Three stages: killing a man for the sake of peace; killing
an animal in order to eat it; finally, eating without killing.

Da capo to the Origin

Even when we are peaceable, which is to say healthy carriers,
all of us transmit original sin. Original, because it corrupted
the first paradise, where everything was good to eat; where
our first parents could eat anything they liked, but for one
thing: they were forbidden to eat the fruit of the tree of
knowledge. Tempted by a serpent, Eve ate the fruit; she
then gave it to Adam, who ate it as well. From the dawn and
genesis of humanity, as if in a loop, there comes back over
and over again this verb: to eat.

Eve ate an apple, from the floral kingdom. Did the first
paradise symbolize the paleolithic era of hunter-gatherers,
in which this first couple, abstaining from the hunt, lived
only on the harvest? The serpent, by contrast, a seducer,
consumed fauna, which is to say other living creatures. He
hunted. He killed in order to eat. Eve, in eating the apple,
refused to kill animate beings. In so doing she turned away
from the properly paradisiacal innocence in which animals
live, creatures that, having no qualms, hunt and kill in order
to eat. Rejecting this virginal guilelessness, and because she

had renounced this innocence, she invented a transgression, an original sin; just so, strictly speaking, she invented the idea of culpability for injury due to willful violence—the essential quality of moral conscience, and perhaps of human consciousness itself. In turning her back on paradise, which is to say on that supralapsarian state in which animals live, she made it possible for human beings to evolve. Even in order to eat, Eve no longer wished to kill: the innocence of wild beasts gave rise to human sin, no matter that we proclaim our innocence in shedding the blood of these blameless creatures. Original sin consisted, literally, in becoming inoffensive. Killing became the major sin, rightly said to be mortal. The manducation of animals assumes and perpetuates this violence, which will never leave us. Leaving paradise behind, becoming human, meant forsaking the murderous innocence of animals. They kill in order to eat. Thou shalt no longer kill, not even in order to eat.

Eve, a gatherer, not a hunter, thus prefigures the Eucharistic manducation of flora: apple, wheat, grape. Eve: no blood in paradise. Jesus: no blood on earth, henceforth, through the Eucharist. Ought we to venerate a Christ-like Eve?

A transhistoric short circuit between two origins, in other words, the one of humanity lost, the other of humanity saved. In this dazzling flash of lightning there also come back to us, after Eve the mother, her son Abel, with his animal offerings, and Cain, his brother, with floral offerings. From the paradise of hunter-gatherers, innocent eaters of beasts, among them a woman who was guilty of eating an apple, there descended the neolithic age of farmers: on the flora side, Cain, farmers; on the fauna side, Abel, breeders. Cain suddenly obstructed historical evolution by killing his shepherd brother, thereby reverting to human sacrifice—while at the same time instituting it?

To sum up. The mother ate the apple; one of her sons sacrificed beasts, the only sacrifices acceptable to the Lord; the other sacrificed his brother. Flora, fauna, man. The long patience of history becomes clear when we consider that, in order for this law of three stages to develop in the right direction from the moment of its embryonic origin, its terms reversed and condensed, it was necessary to wait until Isaac appeared, then Jonah, then the Last Supper: man, fauna, flora—an interval of centuries, no, of millennia.

Are we fully aware of what we do when we eat? Eating, now as always, is a biological necessity; today it has become a political choice, for the sake of saving the planet; but apart from these things, and above all, it is a sacred act. The three major Abrahamic religions celebrate a meal. Peace through and for the Last Supper in common; communion.

A Digression

I marvel at the streamlined torpedo-shaped bodies of fish in the open water, fish whose muscles, nerves, scales, and fins are oriented toward the mouth, frontward, and work solely on its behalf; the act of eating gives purpose to the whole body, itself shaped by the necessity of eating. I marvel also at the bodies of birds, fitted together with a more or less long neck so that the beak projects still further forward. I admire also the bodies of quadrupeds, oriented, like the others, to snout, mouth, and muzzle; and those of crawling serpents, which are nothing but long necks.

When hominids began to walk upright, the mouth, exceptional in this respect, lost its forward position—unique, primordial, essential, vital, inevitable—and became aligned on the same vertical axis with the breasts, knees, and toes. Thus our body lost its old finality, in the Aristotelian sense; we no longer lived solely in order to eat. Manducation remained a necessary human activity, of course, but it was no longer first in the order of life; even so, it was primary in the earliest age of human history—I was about to say, the archaic age.

Once manducation left a space open for it in the mouth, speech descended between the tongue, the lips, and the teeth, from which it then emerged. The hard gave way to the soft, nature gently gave way to supernature—a decisive moment in hominoid development, so solemn that I am not the first to call it sacred.

The word made itself flesh.

The Urge to Belong

In the past we ate among ourselves, as we still often do today, excluding others, for people enjoy the company of people like themselves. Henceforth you shall love one another, for there are no longer others unlike you: in Christ you are all one. Jesus inaugurated a way of living in common in which grace and love dissolve particular attachments. Whoever we may be, without regard for our place of origin or our native language or the foods we are accustomed to eat, we shall eat together.

This new foundation refused to define the individual as someone who, *belonging* to one community, therefore *does not belong to some other community*. Jew or Greek, male or female, slave or free . . . Greek was set apart from Jew, female from male, citizen from slave; feudalism, royalty, the papacy during the Middle Ages, the emirates today—all these were and are matters of family rivalry. The Capulets hated and fought the Montagues; nations declared war upon one

another; churches banished heretics, burned them sometimes, and put unbelievers to death. Nothing has been more
devastating than the urge to belong.

Belonging implies not belonging: there can be no interior
without an exterior; position entails opposition, thesis antithesis, inclusion exclusion. Through this logic of negation,
this turning back at the frontier, the urge to belong gives
birth to mortal struggle, to rivalry, conflict, and death. Let
us, by contrast, imitate the example of the master become
slave, he who was prepared to confront his end up close—as
close up as may be done.

John 4:9–30 relates Jesus's encounter with a woman from
Samaria, near a well famous since the time of Jacob. Here
the frontier reaches higher ground, for it was a matter of
two adorations, one practiced on Mount Gerizim, the other
in the Temple of Jerusalem; the rite was the same, but the
distance between the two was irreducible. The woman who
came to draw water from the well insisted on this difference
in belonging: I am from here, you are from down there.
Jesus replied: the hour is coming when true worshippers will
worship the Father in spirit and in truth. This spiritual truth
will cause the animosities arising from partisan separation to
melt away. Those who receive it will speak in tongues, as if
they emitted sounds that would contain, blend, and bring
together all languages.

And so there appeared a nonbelonging, without partition,
with neither opposition nor exclusion, with neither rivalry
nor dialectic, whose positive nature, far from harming the
stability of the group, makes it possible to strengthen it. Thus
Jesus overruled Hegel.

Religions, through the universality longed for by their adherents, have proved to be more long-lasting than civilizations. Why? Because civilizations, dependent as they are on belonging to a group, develop in opposition to other civilizations, neighboring or remote. Struggle is born of this opposition, and struggle entails death. How could a negative principle of this kind become the driving force of history, the force that propels time forward, when from rivalry, conflict, and combat there comes only death? By killing people and cultures, this negative principle stops time.

The fact that all Churches have committed the sin of rehabilitating various forms of attachment makes it possible to estimate the inertia of group membership and the subterranean force of the urge to belong; but it cannot cancel the primitive and fundamental discovery of the immense benefit to be derived from their disappearance, and the intense desire one day to attain paradise on earth, when there will no longer be any division among peoples.

Let us eat together.

God and True Love
Birth and Genealogy

Violence having been extinguished, what can replace it in order to bring us together? This.

Judaism is presented not only as a religion, the most admirable of all according to its adherents, but also as a genealogy: one becomes a Jewish man or woman by virtue of being born of a Jewish mother. In other words, men and women who no longer believe a word of the Torah and no longer respect the Prophets, even ignore them, will nonetheless remain, and proclaim themselves to be, Israelite, because they descend from a woman issued from the same line. Thus genealogy replaced collective attachments and caused them to enter into nature, into the living world; indeed, placed them at the very heart of life—an innovation that was achieved at the price of restricting God's Covenant to a chosen people.

Christianity, while faithful on the whole to Judaism, departs from it with regard to this fundamental matter, the relationship between a person and a religion. Whoever loses his faith can no longer claim to be a Christian. Why? Because the relationship has been removed from the family, even—an extraordinary step, this—from the mother's womb.

The Holy Family
There are three types of paternity, maternity, and consanguinity: natural, through carnal knowledge; legal, by sworn declaration; and adoptive, by personal choice. In the Holy Family, the father, Joseph, is not the natural father, nor is Jesus the natural son. It is impossible, however, for the mother not to be the mother, for we all come out of a woman's belly. But the new familial arrangement adds a decisive element to the abrogation of natural descent: the virginity of Mary, which, seen in this light, stands out in striking relief and is forever deprived of its impossibility.

On the other hand, the Gospel according to Saint Luke nowhere says that Joseph declared the child's birth to the authorities, even though everyone in those days came to Bethlehem to be counted in the census. On the contrary, terrified by King Herod's order that firstborn male children be killed, the family fled to Egypt.

I note in passing that Herod's massacre of the innocents is rightly seen as part of a body of criminal practices resulting from the importance assigned to consanguinity in social structures and political systems. When political power is transmitted by direct descent, it is wise to kill other heirs in the cradle in order to protect oneself later from a possible rival. In the account of the Nativity, this slaughter creates a sort of figure-ground relationship for the purpose of establishing a new conception of kinship. The old, deadly system provides a tragic setting for the new one.

The Holy Family represented a remarkable innovation, deconstructing the society of the time, founded on family genealogy, and substituting for the natural bonds of kinship the practice of adoption, a custom borrowed from the Romans, based on choice, individual and free, through love. I choose you because I love you. The hard gives way to the soft, nature gently gives way to supernature.

And then the Gospel was announced—in the first place, as an elementary structure of kinship, but, more than this, as an element of all human relations. Love, an essential and universal relation, now constructed relationships for a new world. With the birth of Christ a new era dawned, in which kinship was no longer to have its basis in nature, even from the belly of a woman, but according to the evangelical precept: Love one another. Though naturally and legally you may be father and mother, daughter and son, you will be part of the Christian family only if, in addition, you love one another as individuals. Moreover, and from the point of view of psychology and the human sciences, you will be recognized as parents and your children will be recognized as descendants if and only if each one, freely and individually, chooses the other through love. My dream is that every mother, in the moments after delivery—after the Nativity, I mean—will say to her newborn child, lying naked on her bare belly, and as though in response to its first cries: I recognize you, I had chosen you, you are the one I have so long desired, I adopt you because you are the one whom I love.

Anthropologists tell us that bonds of kinship structure our symbolic thought. Let us once more consider the Holy Family, in which Jesus is not the son and Joseph is not the father. Jesus was not born of Joseph; he is the son of God the Father, to be sure, but it is written (Matthew 1:18, Luke 1:26–28) that his mother conceived by the Holy Spirit; the Scriptures also call him Son of Man. Thus the bond between son and father came to be distended.

But what does it mean to say that a mother remains a virgin? It very frequently happens that a child is born of an unknown father, or of a man who left the mother during her pregnancy or who died; paternity does not acknowledge, at least did not use to acknowledge, tacitly or otherwise, any "natural" rule. Maternity, by contrast, involves something like a universal law, which admits of no exception: a child having no mother is unknown. Now, Mary's virginity introduced a rupture within this law, and a rarity. If consanguinity and paternity are taken away, so is maternity, at least in part, something still more extraordinary. The adjective "holy" in the expression "the Holy Family" therefore signifies that it *undoes* carnal, biological, social, natural, and, as I have said, structural bonds: each in his own way, the father is not a father, nor is the son really a son, nor is the mother truly a mother—a lessening and suppression of blood relations.

This renunciation implicitly nullified the bonds of so-called natural kinship; indeed, John (1:12–13) explicitly speaks of "children of God, who were born, not of blood nor of the will of the flesh nor of the will of man, but of God." Thus the

Gospel, a revelation of love, is communicated to all people, without any distinction being made among them.

Rearing, Education

Parenthetically, this revolution transformed culture since it turned away from nature, by rejecting it. No longer natural, but supernatural. So great was its novelty that it foresaw, and settled, centuries in advance, any number of pointless arguments about marriage, divorce, the family, paternity, and, of particular relevance today, homosexual marriage. It was a question no longer of reducing this union to a man and a woman, sexually, naturally speaking, but of universalizing it, extending it to all those persons who love each other, choose each other, and adopt each other. This question has already been decided for two thousand years.

Opponents of homosexual marriage typically claim that a child can grow up and develop only as a result of the concerted efforts of a man and a woman. Do they forget that for centuries the Church, followed later by the state itself, independently but in imitation of it, established boarding schools for boys, who were brought up by priests and male teachers, and, in parallel with these, separate schools for girls, who were brought up by nuns and female teachers? What is homosexual education if not this? Not so long ago, it will be recalled, when the desirability of coeducation was widely seen to be obvious, these same conservatives, and their predecessors, stridently protested, warning that mixing of the sexes would lead to debauchery. Back then they defended homosexual education!

Physical Sciences and Human Sciences

The laws of the so-called hard sciences describe physical necessities, whereas human laws, it is said, derive only from conventions. With the undoubted exception, I repeat once more, of at least one: no one can fail to be born from the womb of a woman, the place from which all cultures naturally spring. Constructed on this inviolable biological law, consistently or not, are the structures of the family and the laws of kinship, cultural and juridical both, natural, based on blood.

For this physical necessity, which no one can escape, Christianity heroically substitutes the individual liberties of love and choice. Adoptive love is free to determine the structures of kinship as it pleases, not least with regard to maternity. Two parallel dogmas—of the virginal conception of Jesus Christ, the Word of God, and, later, of the Immaculate Conception—located the origin of culture, and therefore of liberty in the face of necessity, in the supernatural. I will come back to this point later.

The Heritage of the Covenant

All of this involves matters of inheritance, without being reducible to it. In the absence of adoptive love and its prerogatives, only male children can inherit. Christianity opened up to all members of the human race, *omnes gentes*, the heritage of the Covenant, reserved by the text that we call the Old *Testament* to family lineages. The New *Testament*, announced by the Archangel Gabriel, bestows this legacy on everyone. It therefore substitutes inclusion for exclusion. The scripture of the modern era *makes its will*, its testament, in favor of all people of all nations, universally.

How could this happen? Through adoption. All people, if they so choose, can become adoptive children of God; the many examples that Christian theology provides them with testify to the dismantling, through adoptive love, of the biological relations of the family, relations of blood and flesh.

At the marriage at Cana, in John 2:4, Jesus asks his mother, "Oh woman, what have you to do with me?" At Matthew 10:37, he says, "He who loves father or mother more than me is not worthy of me; and he who loves son or daughter more than me is not worthy of me." Did Jesus ever speak more clearly?

One of the Gospels begins with Jesus's genealogy (Matthew 1:1–16), tracing his descent through the branches of the tree of Jesse, whereas Jesus himself, in his agony on the cross, transmitted not life through blood, but exactly this election, the choice of all people as the chosen people. Before his suffering and his death, the people gathered on Golgotha had looked upon him in contrast with Barabbas, whose name means "Son of the Father." Jesus's last words (John 19:26–27) were addressed to Mary, his mother, "Woman, behold your son!"—and then to John, his favorite disciple, "Behold your mother!" With his dying breath, the one whom everyone there had distinguished from the Son of the Father transmitted to his favorite disciple, repeating the New Testament, the adoptive bond.

The Elementary Structure of Christian Kinship

For Christianity, love, freely chosen, becomes the sole basis of human relationships, the only true bond. From this followed a rupture with traditional family and tribal relations, and the universal and rational character of the new set of relations, however strange they may have seemed to begin with.

The ordinary elementary structures defined local cultures; their deconstruction, the possibility of choice, the substitution of freedom for necessity in respect of blood relations provided humanity, for the first time, with a universal horizon. The strangeness I just mentioned became *the rational condition of this universality.*

The unique adoptive structure of kinship delivers it from *natural* necessity. But kinship does not therefore become *cultural*, since the free choice of a parental bond depends on neither the languages nor the conventional laws of a given society; no one is prevented from choosing a father, a sister, or a brother from other, distant lineages. Who does not see that racism in all its forms is eradicated by this radical reinterpretation?

The messenger of the Lord announced to Mary that she would conceive through the intercession of the Holy Spirit. This begetting, in other words, being neither natural nor cultural, but angelic, was *spiritual*. What does this last term signify? The sum of the two others and of their negation: the addition of the supernatural and (although no one uses this term) the supercultural; *neither natural nor cultural*. In this way Christianity reconfigured the symbolic meaning of kinship. The universality of the Holy Spirit has its source in this sum of two negations. *Supernatural, which is to say universal.*

The Marian Cult

Someone may object: say what you like about marriage and the adoptive relation, but you cannot maintain that Joseph was not of the male sex and Mary of the female.

My answer is this. The plenary meeting of the bishops of the Catholic Church in France, who form a unisexual society, of men and men alone, not founded on a "natural" family since the participants, all of them celibate, have no children and yet are sometimes called "my father," "my son," and "my brother"—this conference generally takes place at Lourdes, a place where, more than a century and a half ago, Mary herself appeared and said, "I am the Immaculate Conception."

Unjust as a matter of politics and law, odious in the life of business and the professions, often violent in family and private life, always ridiculous and culturally foolish, the pressure exerted by men, I mean males, over women, makes itself felt even in the heavens. In ancient myth, stripping mothers of their procreative function, for no apparent reason and without the least shame, male gods and heroes gave birth to female divinities: thus Zeus, for example, delivered Athena from his forehead, and Adam delivered Eve though his rib. The history of religion, I think I am justified in saying, has not until recently admitted the existence of an exclusively feminine genealogy.

A Feminine Triad

What happened at Lourdes? The Virgin Mary appeared there and declared, in the local patois of Bigorre, to an adolescent shepherdess named Bernadette Soubirous, kneeling before her: "I am the Immaculate Conception." By this Mary meant that from the moment her mother, Anne, conceived her, she was free from original sin. The apocryphal Protoevangelium of James says, moreover, that Anne and her husband Joachim were unable to have a child. Strictly speaking, the miraculous event of her pregnancy has nothing to do with the miracle by which Mary herself conceived Jesus and gave birth to him while remaining a virgin—without a work of the flesh, without Joseph. Indeed, Catholic theology takes care to distinguish the traditional idea of the virginal conception of Jesus, celebrated from the earliest times of Christianity, from the new dogma, enunciated in 1854, and not without controversy, of the Immaculate Conception. Here, then, Mary is speaking, not of her son, but of herself and her mother, Anne.

Suddenly, in 1858, four years after the promulgation of the new dogma, of which Bernadette was wholly unaware, a strikingly novel succession of women illuminated the grotto of Massabielle, just outside Lourdes, on eighteen occasions between February and July: Anne, *absent*, was evoked; her daughter Mary, *appeared*, filled with eloquence; Bernadette, *present*, was silent. This triad connected the elements of a pure genealogy, impeccable in its first link, from Anne to Mary, and spiritual in the second, from the Virgin to Bernadette.

The Mystery of the Trinity
This unanticipated sequence supplied a welcome counter-balance to the machismo of the myths, ancient and false, that I mentioned a moment ago, and qualified the Christian mystery of divine procreation. Here, for the first time, we encounter a feminine trinity by contrast with the canonical trinity in which, without the aid of any woman, without the fecundity of any womb, the line of descent passes through men alone, from God the Father to God the Son; only the Holy Spirit, whose sex is unknown, intervenes. *Genitori geni-toque*, begetter and begotten, in the words of the Eucharistic motet *Tantum ergo*.

The absence of males, of Joachim and, later, of Joseph, the purity of the Virgin, spiritual maternity—here all these things correct, compensate, and redeem the improbable ab-sence of women in the traditional account. Together, the Immaculate Conception and maternal virginity acquire an awe-inspiring force, capable of offsetting the power of the masculine Trinity, itself no less incredible than they are.

Not only a fine equivalence from the spiritual point of view, but a splendid and unexpected reequilibration of justice as well! As inveterate chauvinists, men so little suspected such a symmetry that it long remained incomprehensible to them, no less invisible than Mary's apparition. Whether or not men saw these things as epiphanies, whether or not they believed in them matters little; but were they really incapable of grasping their human—and, dare I say it, biological and spiritual—meaning? Yes, our machismo blinded us to this dazzling truth.

No matter that unbelievers scoff at doubtful miracles and lament the persistence of superstition, pitying the pilgrims who come every year to the grotto, hoping to be cured of illness, the fact remains that ordinary people, more intuitive than the learned, assure, have assured, and no doubt will go on assuring the worldwide and lasting success of Mary's apparitions for an obvious reason: by restoring the feminine element in its just proportion and to its proper place, this rebalancing of the symbolic system of kinship, long overdue, awaited since the dawn of time, in fact, marks the advent of a less violent, less hateful, more peaceable world—in a word, a more feminine world, still far from being realized.

Miraculously prepared more than two thousand years ago by the Gospel text, taught for more than a thousand years by the traditions and theology of the Church, restated by the Virgin more than a century ago and reaffirmed today, the pious dogma of the Immaculate Conception opposed Christianity to anthropology, which is to say the secular attempt to explain the emergence of archaic societies. If you give up anthropology for religion, anthropology will be given back to you a hundred times over.

There is nothing we can do about it. Christianity begot modern society—and this modernity, often without knowing it, perpetuates the fundamental teachings of Christianity, in which love replaces genealogy.

How? By means of biologically (though honestly) false virginities? Such things can be imagined, of course. But can they really be believed?

The contradiction endures. I know it, I think it, and I live it. I am it. I will never be able to leave the Garonne, where I am from, or the religion in which I was brought up, but I also know that I will never come back to places and things that I have left. I believe in God, I do not believe in him. I believe, heads; I do not believe, tails. Heads and tails are sides of the same coin, and I am this coin. *Credo, non credo,* recto and verso, two sides of the same sheet of paper, and I am this sheet. A coin that, thrown in the air, sails, spins, and falls back to earth; a thin leaf sewn in a book, or a delicate leaf on a tree that, alive, quivers in the breeze and that, dead, detached from its branch, floats and tumbles through the air until finally it is laid down on the ground.

No, neither the coin nor the leaf falls at random, for if doubt can lead to faith, faith cannot survive without doubt. They act in concert, just as inhalation and exhalation produce respiration.

Loving may well be easier than believing. But what does it mean to love? Whom are we to love? How are we to love?

What Does It Mean to Love?

Risen from the Dead

Let us consider another honestly false dogma, the dogma of the Resurrection. Believing in this, it has often been objected, leads Christianity into absurdity. How is it that from Saint Paul's time until the present day, billions of human beings have uncomplainingly learned to accept an idea that contradicts both reason and experience? For no one has ever come back from the dead, and no one ever will. And yet, if Christ is not risen, our faith, says Paul, is empty. *Credo quia absurdum*, says Tertullian—I believe because it is absurd.

Here again we must keep in mind two senses of falsehood: one, as in "two plus two equals five"; the other, as in "a fake Vermeer." I call the first "honestly false," for it candidly avows its absurdity; the second I call "dishonestly true," for it tries deceitfully to pass for something it is not. Most of the dogmas of Christianity—Mary's virginity, the resurrection of Christ, the actual presence of his body in the bread of the Eucharist, and so on—are not in any way untruthful, since they frankly present themselves as absurd, impossible, in a word, false. No one has ever known of a child born without the intercession of sperm, no one has ever met a dead person who has come back to life. I therefore call these dogmas honestly false; they wear their falsity on their sleeve for a reason. This is why we must continually *reread* them, in order to discover the profound meaning of their hidden truth, assuming, as one must, that there really is one waiting to be discovered.

Around the tomb, now mysteriously empty, a rock-lined cavity in which the body of the tortured criminal had lain for three days, the first witnesses, women—perhaps only one, Mary Magdalene—claimed to have seen a young man in a white robe (Mark 16:5), or two persons in radiant apparel (Acts 1:10); other accounts report two angels. According to John 20:14–15, Mary turned around and saw Jesus but did not recognize him, believing him to be a gardener.

A little later, two disciples walking on the road to Emmaus met a stranger whom they invited to eat with them, but he vanished the moment they recognized him (Luke 24:31). How could at least one of the two not have identified him at once, since they knew Jesus, knew his voice and his face? According to another account (John 20:24–29), Thomas, one of the twelve apostles, known as Didymus, refused to believe that Jesus had been crucified until he was able actually to touch the scars on his body.

To begin with, then, *no one recognized Jesus.* The canonical texts, clear and transparent, insist on this blindness; they tell of persons who encountered the risen Christ in various guises that hid his identity from them. Once again, where was he? All the Gospel accounts give the same answer: everywhere and right here; he came back, once more incarnate, as anyone at all, a vagrant, a farmer, a stranger, a neighbor. To those closest to him, Jesus appeared as someone unexpected, an ordinary person, a gardener, a traveler, an intruder.

The conclusion is plain: woman or man, rich or poor, white or black, atheist or believer, we are all, virtually, Christ; we all take part in the Incarnation, for he is continually resurrected in each one of us. But the great, the immense difficulty, the almost insurmountable obstacle, in which no doubt the whole apparent contradiction consists, is our not being able to recognize him in the nun, the artisan, the beggar on the sidewalk, the sick person confined to his bed, the madwoman gesticulating wildly, the impotent old man, the ravishingly beautiful young woman, the pole vaulter, the bloody potentate—worse still, in ourselves. He is there, no one sees him. Yet those will be saved who see him, those who know that he shelters them in himself will find happiness and holiness. He is in me, I do not see him. And I will not see you, *I will not love you* so long as I will not have recognized Christ in you, by touching your scars. Love consists in recognizing the divine in another. Paradise is other people, but it goes on being lost, over and over again.

The Resurrection makes it possible to comprehend the meaning of the Gospel, which is to say that which is authentically love; to understand how this love was born, how it became a universal relation. Love is stronger than death, stronger than universal death.

Similarly, in the Eucharist, Christ's body is hidden in the host and his blood in the chalice. They are there, but how are we to recognize them? Resurrection and Real Presence: the same hidden truth, the same secret of love.

The history of the sciences confirms our blindness in the highest degree. Scholarly communities are always slow to recognize innovators, bearers of a transfigured truth—good news, to be sure, but so new that the truth cannot immediately be grasped; these innovators typically die as outcasts, marginal figures, misunderstood, their ideas ridiculed. Generations later, when the evidence accumulated in the interval has changed people's minds, they are rehabilitated, brought back to life, as it were; sometimes they are made into heroic founders, gods of this legend we call history. Or else their successors take all the credit for themselves, acknowledging the discoveries made by others before them while refusing to admit their true authorship, which is kept hidden.

Nothing is more difficult, then, than to detect a new truth beneath the commonplace and the conventional, nothing more difficult than to recognize the Good News.

In much the same way, the biblical kings submitted prophets to torture, sometimes killing them. It must be said that someone claiming to be an innovator or a visionary we are inclined, often rightly, to consider a charlatan. An authentic genius is therefore apt to go unnoticed. Our habitual mistrust, riddled with contradictions, is an endless source of reflection. One thinks in particular of Dostoevsky's story "The Grand Inquisitor": if Christ came back to earth, even the most subtle theologian would show him no welcome, accusing him, not unreasonably, of disturbing social order and encouraging impiety.

We seldom recognize Christ when he appears to us in the guise of our fellow man, often a stranger. Thus Matthew 25:42–43: "For I was hungry and you gave me no food, I was thirsty and you gave me no drink. I was a stranger and you did not welcome me, naked and you did not clothe me, sick and in prison and you did not visit me." I was there, present, risen, not only unrecognizable but unbearable.

We await the Messiah, the King of Glory, says the psalmist. Who today would recognize him in this newborn child, laid down in the straw of a stable between an ox and an ass?

Christ is alive everywhere and in all of us. Yet all of us, even the holiest, are so impure that none of us recognizes him. It may be, I repeat, that Jesus was the only mortal in all of history pure and transparent enough that those who were closest to him, during his lifetime, were able to discover in him the Messiah, the Son of God.

Through the Incarnation and the Trinity, Catholicism is a mono-polytheism, that is, *a synthesis of ordinary religion, found in all societies, and the exceptional religion of the prophets*, a synthesis of anthropology and mysticism. Thus it is distinguished from Judaism and Islam, both obedient to a strict monotheism; Protestantism, for its part, hesitates between the two positions, the one more logical, the other so close to anthropology that it leaves open the possibility of a kind of paganism, but that for this reason is closer to the reality experienced by most human beings, ordinary men and women. With compassion and humanity, Catholicism unites the polytheism of every society with prophetic monotheism, the political with the mystical—I was about to say, the false with the true.

In sum: the communion of saints (*communio sanctorum*) binds together the members of society by means of ceremonies that, while they are certainly liable to produce idols, nonetheless serve to filter out what is false. The Holy Family disavows all allegiance to genealogy in order to announce the Good News, to announce love as a universal relation. Through the Incarnation and the Resurrection, it shows how love can be born in all persons, through the recognition of the divine in others and in ourselves. Without the Resurrection our faith would be empty, because it is through the Resurrection that the dynamic of love stands clearly revealed.

The Light Within

I no longer find the Resurrection either so mysterious or so contradictory as I once did; I have encountered it any number of times in my personal life and in my work as a philosopher. I call it the indefinite, the virtual, the potential, the white space, at once the sum and the concealment of all colors. Radiating throughout the world, it is immense and, at the same time, local. It is widespread among things, even the most innocuous; among living creatures, even the most insignificant; among human beings, even the humblest of them. Its light illuminates everything, but the richness of its colors is hidden beneath its transparency.

A particular individual is defined by an open-ended, in-finite series of properties, which philosophers call accidents; but in every person there exist potentialities that do not be-long to the series. Each person is, of course, the integral of the series; but he or she can become what this virtual nucleus of power promises. In and of themselves they are well de-fined, but all persons carry within themselves this indefinite nucleus of possibilities. You are Catherine, you are Michael, but each of you carries within you a blank page on which the Word writes. In you Christ is continually brought back to life. But he remains buried under these masses of accidents.

It is wrong to say a person is; a person *may be*. Through this indefinite potential, through this virtual nucleus, he or she is Christ arisen. Or rather: this virtual nucleus cease-lessly seeks to bring Christ back to life. But few recognize him in themselves or in others. The virtual is Christ; Christ is the virtual, indefinitely distributed in all of us. Potential, virtual—a word that, literally, signifies our virtue, which is to say our essence, here and now. We are raised up, male and female. We are risen.

Love. I love you if and when I recognize Christ in you, him who has suddenly appeared, like a flash of lightning, raised up from the dead, the darkness of your body, which he makes splendid and luminous. Once he has appeared in you, blessed are you among women. Thus spoke the Archangel Gabriel to Mary (Luke 1:28).

Annunciation and birth. Mary was pure, transparent, filled with grace, to such a degree that God himself, God the Father, was with her: *Dominus tecum*. When the Arch-angel Gabriel appeared to her, he understood that the Lord was with her—not only with her, but in her, and for her, so

much so that his Son was made incarnate in her flesh, as if
the Father conceived his Son in her through the working
of the Holy Spirit. Everyone has met women so saintly that
they, likewise blessed among all women, are impregnated
with the Lord. As the fruit of Mary's womb himself did, they
save human beings. Mary Magdalene was also pure enough
to recognize the One who had arisen.

Incarnation. Jesus was no doubt the purest man who
ever lived, in whom love was so transparent that the smallest children recognized him as Christ—more readily in any
case than sages and savants, many of whom have failed to
recognize him at all.

God, it is said in Genesis, created man in his image. Every
person therefore carries within himself a reflection of the
divine and, potentially at least, is radiant with it; for each
person filters this light, or hides it, or lets it shine through.
The virtual, lacking flesh, is unrecognizable. The Gospels
complete the Old Testament by combining this image with
the idea of a Real Presence. The Resurrection makes Christ
live and relive in us. We hide him, filter him, let him appear.
We recognize him in another person, we see him corporeally, in the bearing, the gaze, gestures, words, and acts of
another—not only the image of Christ, but the model himself. The Gospel incarnates Genesis, sings of its blossoming.

Life. I will exist only when Christ is reborn in me. *Dominus mecum.*

Foods. I will truly live when I recognize Christ in the
bread and the wine. The secret of the Resurrection lies already in the Eucharist. When you eat bread, when you do
the most common, everyday things, I will be in you, I will
be brought back to life in you. When you drink wine, I will
reappear, I will circulate among you, like blood in the body.

What wine flows in the blood of the one I love, how much bread is there in the flesh of one who has been tortured?

Death and resurrection. I will no longer fear death once the Risen Lord lives in me.

A dead man is brought back to life. From this vital, supremely honest untruth emanates the miracle of love.

Love Spoken on a Blank Page

Caught up in these rare ecstasies, mischievousness catches me unawares—also the smiling model of what might be called the infinitesimal silence of the cause and the unbearable lightness of the truth. In the most inspired love letter ever composed by a male hand, Diderot wrote this to Sophie Volland: "I waited for you; you didn't come; I must leave; night has come, darkness falls. I cannot see what I am writing, I do not even know if I am writing; and so wherever you see nothing written down, read that I love you." Ever since first reading these sublime lines, I have scarcely dared to write! And yet I dream of occupying the place of Diderot, the lover who expresses himself so attractively; still more would I like to be in the place of his beloved Sophie: everywhere I see nothing written down, I hope to read that someone loves me.

Better free choice than vital necessity—thus the definition of love. From this follow two more questions.

Whom Are We to Love?

Glory or Peace?

Glory holds the members of a group together, crystallizes their relations with one another, binds them to one another. Glory to Lady Di and to Johnny, stereotypical stars of popular culture, embodiments of the three forces—money, sex, and power—that drive us forward in the hope of attaining this supreme end for ourselves. Each of us seeks to win, to finish first, to become more powerful; everyone seeks glory for himself, denying it to others, who become rivals. Our relations burst into flame, as on a battlefield; the war of all against all spills over into the whole web of relations—money, science, language, religion. No opportunity is missed to gain advantage in reaching the apex of a cone, the summit of a pyramid before anyone else. The unquenchable thirst for glory reinstitutes hierarchies; the sorrows of the world derive from just this. No more love, consequently no more joy.

The poison of glory has spawned resentment on a vast scale, causing wars and the death of human beings in great numbers: thousands in the case of Caesar and Louis XIV; tens and hundreds of thousands in the case of Napoleon and Pol Pot; millions in the case of Hitler, Stalin, and Mao. The historical glory of these killers depends on the forgetting of so many unknown cadavers, who can be remembered only if we read history upside down, which is to say right side up: by adopting the point of view of the victims.

So long as each person seeks to win renown for himself, we will not live in peace. If I praise one without praising the other, there will be no end to rivalry. The old gods themselves were rivals, constantly at war with one another; the false ones are recognized by their human, all too human behavior. Of whom, then, does the Gloria sing? "Glory to God in the highest, and on earth peace to men of good will."

The angels, having suddenly been superseded by Christ the Mediator, brought into the world that night, in Bethlehem, in a stable, had therefore lost their usefulness in conveying messages and establishing relations among men; on leaving the stage of the world, the angels, formerly intermediaries and mediums, sang the praises of the Lord so loudly that the intensity of the musical wave they sent forth reached an immense height, the distance separating the earth, here below, from the heavens, from the Lord Most High; it precisely measured, in other words, the infinite distance between the immanent and the transcendent, along a vertical axis.

Let us suppose, then, that true glory lives *up there, very high—so high that nothing is more inaccessible than this summit*: beyond the reach of magnificent ceremonies, so high up that none among us will ever be able to reach it. For the ridiculously low apexes of our cones of glory remain always accessible; wealth and royalty are located at a finite distance from us. If, to the contrary, no one were to consume the intoxicating drug of earthly fame, we would no longer have to fight over it, all against all. So long as the apex of a cone, the top of a pyramid, is a finite distance from its base, many, if not all, people will desire to reach it; but if the distance is too great, if no one can reach it, then we are saved—no more invidious comparison, no more jealousy and rivalry, no more of this hatred that leads us to massacre one another, until finally no one will be left. No more war. Peace. Love. The cone, now empty, disappears; a new web takes its place, another universal relation, the communion of saints—the spiritual union of the members of the Catholic Church, past and present.

Praise

To avoid the prospect of total war, then, and the possible extinction of the human race, glory must be given only to *Him than whom no one else is higher*. This title, Most High, aligns the scale of comparison vertically, while emptying it of all gradations, as though the rungs of a ladder were ripped out; it designates the One who occupies its apex, infinitely far from us. Let us therefore praise *Him who, by taking upon Himself, Most High, the totality of human envies, loves, and hatreds, abolishes our rivalries in their entirety.* Let us praise *Him in relation to whom no comparison is possible.* Henceforth, comparison is useless.

Let us never praise, in this world below, any great king, any great power or majesty, any conquering general who has sent thousands to their death on a field of battle, whose crime will be repaid in the coin of vengeance, tomorrow, by the vanquished; indeed, any gaudy nonentity photographed by the media whose image turns up today on our screens, perched on a ladder of comparison from which, tomorrow, he is almost certainly to fall. Let us praise instead *Him in whom the ladder of rivalry vanishes.* To You alone the power and the glory. In You, as in a black hole, all our envies disappear; as from a white fountain, all our loves will come from You. Once the mortal poison of glory will have been borne away from us, carried off to infinitely inaccessible heights, we will live in peace.

Let us praise, then, two persons. In the first place, Him who is absent from this world, independent of any ladder, at the infinite limit of its missing rungs. Neither a prince nor a man of power, He is yet so high that He is not among us. As for him who is present in this world, the Messiah incarnate, descended from on high, let us also praise him, because, at the bottom of the ladder, he found there was no room for him at the inn; because he was born in the straw of the stable, in the company of an ox and an ass; because, his family having fled to Egypt in order to prevent him from being killed, he was not counted in the census; absent from official records, he was mentioned by no historian later—he was too lowly.

Classless, unclassifiable, he wandered for three years with no fixed domicile, in the company of other itinerants, fishermen, adulterers, prostitutes. He ended up between two thieves, sentenced to unspeakable torture. Yes, let us praise this one as well, him who is beyond all comparison, at the very bottom of the hierarchy. *No one envied or wished this wasted life for himself.*

His world is not that of our petty kingdoms. The Father reigns on high, Most High; the Son lies far below, at the very bottom. Let us therefore praise the Most High and the most low, for they are one and the same; let us praise this Absent One and this present one, one and the same; both invite us, too far from the one and too near to the other, to live in a world between, pacified by these two intervals. Infinitely high, infinitely low: our praise binds together these two infinites. Rather than behave in destructive ways, abandoning ourselves to criticism, suspicion, and indignation, let us learn that there is no work more useful to our survival than to devote our lives, as nuns and monks have always done, as Johann Sebastian Bach did, to this praise. *Magnificat anima mea.* The joy of praise expands and enlarges our souls, which thus become as inventive as the universe and life; our joy spreads everywhere, among all things and all beings, in all their relations. *Gloria in excelsis Deo*: from our earthly mouths, our music rises to an inaccessible height. Peace on our lowly earth, at last. *Pax hominibus.*

Thus the angels sing, of an unexpected time, a new type of relation, the gospel of love. "See how they love one another," it was said of the first Christian gatherings. Since then, with a kiss or a handshake, they have given to one another the peace of Christ.

How Are We to Love?
Prepositions

By what roads must we travel in order to reach this love? How are we to love, in what manner? By taking all the directions indicated on road signs, where we read: *to, toward, in, from, through, for, between, according to, following, concerning, against, with, among, before, after, while, during* . . . I love you through you, for you, toward you . . . Each preposition points to one or several routes, follows the streams that cross them and that unite all these prepositions, in space, here and elsewhere, in time, past, future, and present, and, cognitively, composition, opposition, classification, evolution . . . The web that these prepositions form, together with conjugations and declensions, their accomplices, give language fluidity, movement, enable it to be adapted to reality; these prepositions relax the fabric of reality, liquefy it, modulate it, aerate it, set it ablaze. Neurobiologists tell us that the brain itself is a dynamic, plastic, staggeringly complex network of neural connections. I love you in every imaginable way.

When philosophers think in terms of concepts—being and time, matter and memory, words and things, difference and repetition—they transform human beings, living creatures, and the objects of the world into marble statuary. They express themselves in the old telegraphic style, which quite rightly eliminated declensions and prepositions for the sake of compression and rapid comprehension. But it is exactly these declensions and prepositions that change the abstract and marmoreal statues of the philosophers into streaming air waves, breaking waves of water, dancing flames; thanks to these things, which soften reality and give it meaning, or at least direction, every language throws itself into the dance of the world and its transformations, brilliant, randomly crackling flames. In speaking and writing, not only do we inundate things with waves, we also illuminate them by the blazing light of an inferno. Mysticism burns with its ecstatic flames.

In a text that bears comparison with Pascal's *Memorial*, Kierkegaard was consumed by these same flames:

> 19 May 1838, 10:30 a.m. . . . an indescribable joy . . . I rejoice in my joy, *of, with, at, for, through, and with* my joy . . . There is an indescribable joy that is kindled in us just as inexplicably as the apostle's unmotivated exclamation: "Rejoice, and again I say, Rejoice" [Philippians 4:4]—Not a joy over this or that, but a full-bodied shout of the soul "with tongue and mouth and from the bottom of the heart": "I rejoice in my joy, of, with, at, for, through, and with my joy"—a heavenly refrain which suddenly interrupts our other songs, a joy which like a breath of fresh air cools and refreshes, a puff from the trade winds which blows across the plains of Mamre to the eternal mansions.
>
> *Journals* II A 228

The Latin Mass indicates a similar route, similarly marked off:

> *Per* ipsum et *cum* ipso et *in* ipso
> Est tibi Patri omnipotenti
> *In* unitate spiritu sancti
> Omnis honor et gloria
> *Per* omnia saecula saeculorum.

> *Through* him, and *with* him, and *in* him,
> O God, almighty Father,

In the unity of the Holy Spirit
All glory and honor is yours,
*For*ever and ever. Amen.

The Universal Web of Relations

Both Kierkegaard, a Protestant, and the Catholic rite draw
upon a set of prepositions in order to describe, on the one
hand, the ecstatic joy experienced in and through our personal
relationship to God, and, on the other, our collective relationship with God in his unitary multiplicity and his trinitarian
unity. There, love fills the individual to overflowing; here, God
occupies him completely. There, joy spreads throughout the
universal web of relations; here, God spins the web.

We never love partially. It is always all or nothing: God
and myself, God and my neighbor; by all ways, by all means,
in every manner. The mother/daughter and mother/son
relations describe, not maternal and filial love, but a pathological situation. If I love you, you are my mother, my sister,
my daughter, my mistress, a stranger—distant, yet so close
that no one has ever been closer to me; you are others, living creatures, the world, with no exception. Love pervades,
permeates the universal web of relations, with no gaps or
breaks. In order to express itself, love needs all prepositions,
not omitting a single one.

Why do I call this universal web of relations religious? Because, in this case, an external object, more or less known,
unknown, misunderstood, an object thrown ahead, though
sometimes it may be an absent, ubiquitous, transcendent
subject—this object/subject binds individuals together in
immanence, so securely that they withdraw as far as possible
into their subjectivity in order to detect in it, from within, the

object/subject that is the most external to it, infinitely distant, God himself. This subjective/objective relation, more or less cognitive in character, acting upon individual persons, brings into existence long-lasting communities. I love you in, through, and for the communion of saints.

Believing in, Believing
The Prepositions of Belief

I believe *in* God, I believe *in* the reality of the external world; I believe what you tell me. Again, let us be attentive to prepositions, which is to say to relations. The preposition *in* or *into* indicates a bath, an immersion, a medium, a milieu, an abode or dwelling; the preposition *to* (in French, *à* may also mean *in*, as in the case of belief) calls to mind an arrow that flies from a subject to its object, a vector that links two definite authorities, different and separate. Where a preposition is absent, the grammar consists of a transitive verb and its complement, a direct object.

Credo in unum Deum . . . The opening words of the Nicene Creed expose and hide two secrets. I have already mentioned the first of these: the initial word, *ego*, is absent; it is implicit, however, in *credo*, the first-person present-tense form of the Latin verb. In affirming this belief and weakening particular attachments, Christianity invented the self. *I* believe.

The second secret plunges *me* into a medium or milieu, a new habitat, God himself: the air that I breathe, the water in which I float and swim, the earth that supports and nourishes me, the fire that illuminates and that warms me, the roof over my head, my neighbors, others whom I meet. When I say "my house," "my neighbors," and so on, I refer to the synthesis that creates an overarching self. I am, in other words, a synthesis that inhabits a Synthesis. Being *of* the world—another way of saying: being *in* God.

Faith, if I may say so, therefore counts for less than this immersion in an environment. What does my belief matter, since I live *in* God as a fish lives in the water? I do not at all believe *in* God; otherwise I would be a subject in the presence of a limited, dominated object, the object of my knowledge and my acts, considered purely in the abstract, without either context or global synthesis, an object whose being or nothingness could be endlessly demonstrated and refuted. Nor do I believe God either; tacit, hidden, invisible, He removes himself from my hearing, from all my faculties of perception.

The Nicene Creed says *Credo in*—I believe *in*—the three persons of the Holy Trinity, Father, Son, and Holy Spirit; but in the case of the Church it omits the preposition, restricting itself to the direct object (*Et unam, sanctam, catholicam et apostolicam Ecclesiam*), the objective and collective rock that *we* ceaselessly help to build. I believe the Church. Continuing in an entirely different register, *Credo* gives way to *Confiteor* ("I confess") and *Expecto* ("I look forward"). Faith ends up in hope.

Dwelling

Thus religion constructs such a house for us to live in that we have no need of any other; all our needs are satisfied there. We dwell in its comfort, its completeness, and its beauty; were we to abandon it, we would weep bitterly, for we have never known how or been able to construct a more perfect home. This is why, in our humility, we cannot believe ourselves to be either its designers or its builders.

An inn for weary travelers; a restaurant where bread and wine are served; a school for novices and catechumens;

a tribunal for confessions of sin, professions of faith, and the Last Judgment, for merits, offerings, and indulgences; a residence for legislators and representatives; a post office for messages where angels bustle about; a meeting place for celebrating births and marriages, for praying against terminal illnesses, for funerals; even a cemetery; a hall of departures and arrivals—this universal house brings together all others, which the city disperses (I was about to say, analyzes). For this same reason the city can also become a prison, for life, for the community, and for thought.

In sum, I am this unity that dwells in Unity, in religion and in the world.

Distant or Near?

Walking along a road, in search of this unity, I approach a mile marker. In order to reach it, obviously I must cover half the distance separating me from it; having done this, I resume my journey, which must now cover the remaining half. But the situation is unchanged: no matter how small the distance yet to be traveled, there will always be a midpoint needing to be crossed. Reason has rigorously and unfailingly demonstrated, at least since the time of Zeno of Elea, that no matter how many times I succeed in cutting the remaining distance in half, there will always remain a tiny interval left to be traversed, and I will never arrive at my destination. Yet in fact I do get there eventually, in defiance of all understanding.

On the one hand, I am still infinitely far from my destination; on the other, I have reached it with no trouble at all, by somehow leaping over the infinitely short remaining distances—as if my legs had paid no attention to Zeno's proof. No: as if body and soul, by a concerted effort, had blithely disposed of the contradiction.

Overstepping the rational limit, a short circuit suddenly explodes into whiteness, light, perfect joy.

A Mathematical Digression

Measure a length, a surface, or a volume as precisely as you like, to within a centimeter, a millimeter, an angstrom . . .—no matter how accurate it may be, your measurement will never attain the abstract perfection of the geometric straight line. The same will be true for the area of a triangle or the volume of a regular polyhedron. No matter how accurate your approximation, no matter that it comes infinitely near to the abstract figure, it will nonetheless remain infinitely far from it. This is the same paradox as Zeno's.

The infinite distance and the infinite nearness of God are neither more nor less thinkable than the fact that the distance between numerically exact physical measurements and geometric perfection is both infinitely great and infinitely small. In both cases, another world is unveiled. Recall what I said earlier about Kojève's idea, that mathematical physics could have emerged in Galileo's time only through a short circuit between these two distances, one infinitely great, the other infinitely small.

Although it verges on the miraculous, the two may therefore be put into relation with each other. Religion binds them together.

Return to Religion

When I was young, faith offered me easy access to God. Honesty led me to travel a long and hard road of rational knowledge and human loves. Now, near the end of my life, and still not done with thinking about death, I find myself infinitely far from the hoped-for threshold, frozen in place despite my great strides. My detours have not brought me an inch closer; I remain as before, both mobile and immobile, at an infinite distance from my goal, separated by a gap that is both unimaginably wide and unimaginably narrow; even so, I find myself as near as possible to the end point, in its infinitely immediate vicinity.

Infinitely near, infinitely far—*they are the same but for the sign*. Journey without end, an end that is instantaneously reached. Darkness and light, open and closed, one and the same moment. If I were to write a thousand pages more, there would be a thousand more left to write; another thousand after that and still I would not be any closer to being done; or, rather, I would still be, whether running forward or running in place, as close as ever. I believe, I do not believe, almost at the same time. Faith and doubt, the false and the true are telescoped in these two infinites.

This is why only one of the inventors of the infinitesimal calculus—which, for the first time and by means of a definite integral, delivered reason from Zeno's prison—only one of them, Pascal, could have written, thinking of Jesus: "You would not look for me if you had not already found me."

Here I am, infinitely far from God, who is absent, but infinitely near to God, who is everywhere. The ultimate decision, the choice, the turning point, arriving at the limit, at the end—do these things lie inside me? No. Through grace and invention, they lie outside of me. Who therefore will open the door? Alone, I cannot. Pascal does not say "I," he says "you." The one who continues on his way is not the one we think it is; he is the one to whom God speaks. O Lord, You see that I am looking for You; please open the door that my reason has closed, at once!

Wandering, weeping, I await the change of sign. Hope takes the place of faith, whose distance from reason is now reduced to an infinitely small gap. The leap, the bridge from one to the other, which ten sages say must be crossed in order to enter heaven, requires but a small bound.

I used to think of myself as a fragment thrown out at random, a leaf in the wind; now I find myself instead standing on the threshold and yet infinitely far from it. Must I start all over again?

For I live infinitely far from You (you), but infinitely near; for You (you) are infinitely near me, but infinitely far.

Love, divine and human, binds these two infinites together.

CHAPTER 3

THE PROBLEM OF EVIL

Parts and Totalities

I would not have dared to write a book on religion out of anxiety or hope alone, powerful though these two emotions are. I was also motivated by a desire to go on constructing, blindly, as I have done from the beginning, a synthetic philosophy. Along the way, cultural shifts and changing styles of thinking led me to wonder whether this way of proceeding might not one day come to take precedence over the analytic tradition, which had now become partial, ineffective, even counterproductive. Analysis is critical and regressive; it undoes and destroys. Synthesis, by contrast, through the sort of organic linkages, both local and broad, that I had managed to detect in a series of books—from *Hermès* (5 vols, 1969–1980) to *Hominescence: Le Grand Récit* (2001), from *Interférence* (1972) to *Hermaphrodite* (1987), from *La Légende des Anges* (1993) to *L'Art des Ponts Ponts* (2006)—is progressive and constructive. *Le Passage du Nord-Ouest*

(1980) linked the oceans and the sciences; *Le Contrat naturel* (1990) connected human beings with the world.

Approaching the end of this vast project, how could I not turn to religion, inasmuch as it too brings a great many elements together and from them synthesizes a totality, similar not only to the one that the sciences explore and explain, but also to the one that every philosophy is bound to patiently construct, piece by piece? Before describing these totalities and noticing their resemblances, let us look at the parts of which they are composed.

Partitions on a Map of the World

On the map, as in reality, France is divided from Spain by the barrier of the Pyrenees, from Italy by the Alps, from England by the Channel, and from Germany by the Rhine; but only our whims, our history, and our politics divided the Mediterranean into Ionian, Tyrrhenian, and Adriatic seas. To the east and the west they are the same waters, fed by the currents of the Atlantic, which in turn are variously mixed and mingled with those of the other oceans. Communicating with one another by the three great southerly capes and by the northwest passage through the Arctic, these oceans constitute a universal of waters: a million sites, everywhere the same fluid.

Similarly, every class or moment of the philosophical totality I have been constructing combines elements of scholarship and worship, both totalities themselves, as if the one were spread distributively in the other. My first book, an examination of Leibniz's mathematical system, concluded by paying tribute to the scientific works of Pascal, who recognized Christ as the fixed point missing from Leibniz's exact and rigorous formulations. *La Parasite* (1980) reread the story of Joseph. *La Légende des Anges* followed on from *Hermès*. *Rome* (1983) considered the Lord's Prayer ("Our Father who art in heaven . . .") in connection with Jupiter. My reading of the novels of Jules Verne (2003) concluded with a rereading of the Book of Exodus. *Le Contrat naturel* culminates in a celebration of the Earth in the form of litanies. *Le Tiers-Instruit* (1991), at the end, sings the Song of Mary, the Magnificat. *Rameaux* (2004) is devoted to the life and works of Saint Paul. *Statues* (1987) closes in ecstasy before the manger. *Musique* (2011) contemplates the prenatal Visitation of the Virgin Mary to Elizabeth. In short, the totality of religion is distributed in parts, each one itself a totality, in the philosophical synthesis under construction, drawing upon the encyclopedia of the sciences. I would have been able, in other words, to write a book on religion by taking these total parts one by one.

My task in the present book was therefore to discover a sort of reciprocity through which the scientific and philosophical totalities, distributed in their turn in total parts, is found in the totality of religion. Accordingly, the reader has been able to revisit some of the arguments I developed in *Les origines de la géométrie* (1993) and consider information theory, the theory of evolution, and chaos theory in the context of an anthropology and a philosophy of history. The three totalities encompass one another, intertwine and penetrate one another; global oceans and local seas, everywhere a single fluid swept along by interacting marine currents.

Since any particular line meets every other line in it, the network of total parts represents the world, this viscous kingdom, like a formal model, but in a solid state. The bonds of the preceding chapters, vertical and horizontal, respectively, form the warp and weft of this network.

Another Image of Total Parts

In its phenotype and genotype, through its environment and evolution, every organism contains within itself the presence, proximity, or trace of other living creatures and the world. It is as though a species such as ours draws a weft yarn through innumerable warp yarns, sometimes through all of them. In this way the community of living creatures and the whole of the inert world come to be obliquely projected on the human organism, a new total part.

The classification of totalities I have just sketched thus takes in not only the terrestrial gown of the seas and the floating scarf of the air, but also what I have called the biogea, the swarms of living things that inhabit and cover our planet.

Lacunae

The philosophical totality, as I have blindly constructed it, has so far failed to take into account politics and religion. A few of my writings dealing with aspects of ecology, law, and current events have called attention to the need to devise a new politics—a matter of great urgency at a time when our outmoded forms of government are incapable of coping with the novel challenges of a world they neither built nor foresaw.

I have therefore wished to complete this program before I die, by rereading the religions of my culture, Greco-Roman paganism, Judaism, and Christianity. Hence the present book. I miss the religion of my adolescence; I remain inconsolable at having lost it, through my head. Nevertheless it has lived on in my life and how I have tried to live my life. How can I repay Christianity, at least in the small and humble coin that is all I have to give, for the treasures that gladdened me when I was young?

Cognitive Dualism

Answering this question, already too personal a question, forces me to come to terms with an entirely different totality: a subjective synthesis.

Accustomed as we are to separate the soul from the body, we live and think as dualists, ignoring the protests of our own souls and our own bodies. When we describe a person's relations to things and with others, we speak in terms either of the intellect or of the heart, which we call the seat of the emotions and sentiments. At the top, moving, neurons in the head; lower down, moved, mediastinum and intestine. Colds from knowing, fevers from feeling. The intestine thinks as much as the cortex; besides, as I have said more than once, I write with my feet.

When we describe religions we remain prisoners of this dualism. Either we debate theological questions dialectically, using rational arguments, or we pour out our feelings: either the God of philosophers and scholars or the God, softer hearted, of Abraham, Isaac, and Jacob.

But religious persons, for the most part, speak neither of reason nor of the Pascalian heart dear to Rousseau and like-minded sentimentalists; without speaking of them, some may nonetheless embrace both, others neither one. What name shall we give to a third impulse, also unspoken, yet encouraged by all the cultures of the world? Through weavings of warp and weft, webs of relations, and distributed totalities, it lives constantly in globality, as much in the rational mode of formal inquiry as in the emotional mode of anxiety and gaiety, and indeed in other modes as well. Believing *in*, as I said earlier, is an immersion involving this third impulse, integral and synthetic—an impulse itself immersed in a synthetic and integral globality. How does this existential function operate?

Audio musicam ergo sum

Music supplies us with a first clue. What part of me hears music when I listen to it? My body trembles, dances, kicks up its heels, perhaps jumps with joy; music innervates and stretches the muscles, accelerates the pulse, moves the stomach and stimulates the genitals. My intellect counts, unconsciously, admiring the harmonic composition and construction of counterpoint. My hearing, in its delight, floods the whole sensory system with musical waves; inner rhythms and tempos keep time with the same metronome. My feelings move me to tears and fill me with happiness—all these bonds, suddenly global, construct my unity.

No part of me is unaffected by the mute ecstasy that listening to music induces. Music seizes me, holds me spellbound, passes through me, possesses me, makes me all its own, causes some unknown federative and existential function to operate in me, unifying the integral of what I am, like an immense embrace—this intense ecstasy that is called existence.

I listen to music, therefore I am.

Subjective, Objective, Cognitive, and Collective

Looked at another way, music unites choir, soloist, and orchestra; accompanies a corps de ballet; precedes a company of marching soldiers; prompts communicants to stand up and extend their hands; serenades waltzing couples on skates, holding each other tight as they glide over the ice . . . Music federates the subjective, body and soul; the objective, copper, wood, chords, and waves; the cognitive, artistic composition and aesthetic appreciation; and, finally, the collective, carried away by its rhythms and charmed by its melodies. No one can dance faster than the music, as the proverb has it. This means that it comes before all things, including the harmony of the heavenly bodies and the sentences that I write down. None of the other arts manages to bring about—in me, in us, everywhere—a more united federation, a more complete synthesis, a more total totality.

Dualists as we still are, we speak of the history and theory of music, of the fugue, of composers and instruments, and we praise the emotions that music arouses. We think about music in terms of reason or the heart, one or the other, but not both. Is it, then, really a question of what I hear, the person to whom the composer and the performer speak? Or is it a question of something prior, a fundamental anteriority, which music represents and sets in motion and guides us toward? A similar distinction obtains in the case of the religious person, one who worships. We are still captivated by the urge to analyze, to distinguish, separate: release and imprisonment, light and pollution.

The Father and the Day

Earlier I mentioned Jupiter, whose name (combining day and father) signifies the synthesis of our physical knowledge of light and the altogether human emotion associated with filiation. The same synthesis is found in "Our Father, who art in heaven . . . ," except that this formulation adds both a collective dimension, referring to us, human beings, and an existential dimension, expressed by the verb "to be." Whence the question, implied in the one case by a single word and in the other by six words: how can it be that, under skies that bathe us in light, I maintain a relationship with my and our father of submission and love that not only psychology and sociology but also anthropology and politics describe, each in its own way? As strange as it may seem, we are immediately

obliged, in asking this, to inquire into the nature of our existence, physical and social alike—an inquiry that is neither
rational nor affective, but that nonetheless involves both reason and the emotions, and something else as well.

Where, then, does religion come from? Having some
knowledge of astronomy and electrostatics, I am well aware
that no one is hurling thunderbolts from behind the clouds
with the intention of illuminating, warning, or wounding;
well aware, too, from what the human sciences have taught
me about the bonds between father and son, of the inanity
of this supernatural creature of our fantasies. Undermined
on both sides—by the sciences and by the humanities, two
partial and complementary points of view—why, one may
wonder, has religion not completely collapsed? The critique
first developed by the thinkers of the Enlightenment, and
then extended by scholars in the twentieth century, has accustomed us to live, for the first time in human history, in
an atheistic culture, delivered at last from absurd imaginings
and illusory terrors.

None of these disciplines, hard or soft, separated by analysis, inquires into the global bond, the existential synthesis
through which every human relationship has its natural place.
Why then do we love one another in this world? Why do
we hate one another, by land and by sea? Why do we live
together, loving plants and animals, once devoured by the
latter, nourished still by the former, in this tiny corner of
a menacing and constellated universe? Religions, synthetic
rather than analytic, have tried to answer universal questions.
Not only do they link together, they bind together.

This existential function, a sort of overture to synthesis,
inevitably leads us to pose deep questions whose answers are
undecidable. It persuades us to construct the world we dwell

in, indissolubly natural and human; it builds the house we live in. This synthesis is what makes us what we are: without it we would have no place to live.

Sciences and religions are distinguished not only by the answers they give to these questions of why and how, but also by the manner in which they answer them, on the one hand by carving up reality, which is apprehended through partial cognitive functions, and, on the other, by means of a global explanation, an overall reckoning. Either we know definite objects analytically, standing back a certain distance from them—believing *to*, as it were (in French, *croire à*), like the arrow that flies from a subject to its object—or we dwell, one and all, in a common mansion whose many passageways we do not entirely perceive—believing *in* (*croire en*). Either things or the world; either myself in pieces or myself whole. Either analysis or synthesis; either untying or tying together.

Deciding

The heart and reason lead us in the direction of the decidable: joy or sorrow, worry or serenity, on the one hand, true or false, just or unjust, residues of the principle of excluded middle, on the other. Through the heart, we laugh and cry; reason, by contrast, analyzes in order to arrive at certainty, sorting truth from error. We demonstrate, experiment, take stock, and, as a result, we decide—as though with a chisel (both words come from the Latin word meaning "to cut off"). We find it so hard to resist the vocabulary of analysis that we hesitate to speak or think otherwise. Yet many inventions, and not the least ones, have come from this "otherwise"; one thinks in particular of the discovery of irrational numbers, non-Euclidean geometries, and quantum mechanics.

For synthesis plunges us and lodges us, apparently in proportion to its scope, in the increasingly undecidable, in the unbearable disequilibrium of the included middle. We decide in order to act and to think locally, in the world around us, which we are able to understand; we dwell in a far vaster world, the global, which surpasses our understanding.

We preserve this dualism in our educational system: on the one hand, the humanities; on the other, the so-called hard sciences, which we separate from the social sciences, even if it means condemning whole generations to understanding nothing of the world in its totality, uncultivated savants and cultivated ignoramuses. We seek to encourage original thinking and boundless curiosity. The problem is that physicians and jurists must be able not only to draw upon a more or less general body of learning, but also to examine individual cases—as if they had two heads; otherwise they will never acquire the broad knowledge of the world their work requires. I have long hoped to see the emergence of bicephaly in this sense, a new kind of bicameral brain!

End of the Analytical Age

The dualism I decry arises from the analytic ideal that has oriented our thinking ever since the dawn of Greek philosophy: dichotomy in Plato, division of difficulties in Descartes. At the outset of the present work I announced the end of this era and the advent of an age in which syntheses, linkages and connections, networks and webs of all kinds will govern our thinking and our behavior.

Why? Because all the problems we face today cut across a great many separate fields—across academic disciplines, business and the professions, departments of government—and can be solved only in a concerted fashion, taking into account divergent opinions and harnessing a variety of technical skills and conceptual approaches, under the guidance of expert negotiators trained in this novel way of thinking. Thus the art of weaving, of tying together, will soon replace the disjunctive and divisive methods of analysis. Hermes's staff, the caduceus, pictures an entwining.

Cutting up destroys, binding together constructs. The extermination of species, climate change, global pollution all derive from this obsession with taking apart, breaking into pieces, distilling mixtures and separating compounds; they derive from solution, in the literal sense, which is to say dissolution, leaving behind a crumbling world, an ocean of waste.

The twilight of demolition, the dawn of building. Protecting the world, this is the task that awaits us.

The Two Metas

Ancient librarians are said to have given the title *Metaphysics* to the works by Aristotle preceding and following the ones on physics. To my way of thinking, this happy accident might have been usefully repeated if they had thought to give the title *Metanomics* to works that might have come before or after the ones he wrote on the constitution of Athens, ethics, and rhetoric—fertile rudiments of what we are now accustomed to call the human sciences. Just as the hard sciences are completed by the treatise on metaphysics, whose questions, bearing on matter, form, time, the universe, and so on, because they are not amenable to experiment, have aroused responses as varied as they are undecidable, so the soft sciences have been obliged to devise, no less modestly, a parallel line of inquiry concerning the individual, history, and human destiny.

The set of questions stated in these two frameworks, now combined and securely bound together, since the destiny of human beings is in no way separate from that of nature, has received a variety of undecidable answers (totemism, animism, polytheism, monotheism, and so on) in all cultures, answers so necessary to their survival, it would appear, and also so universal that I find it impossible to believe that cognition, perhaps human existence itself, does not contain a special function that brings it into contact with the subject matter of metaphysics and metanomics, neither rational nor sentimental but, to the contrary, at once emotive and formal, objective, subjective, collective, and cognitive. Earlier I noted that the monotheism I know best, Catholicism, carries within itself, more or less, all of the answers that I have just mentioned; and I gladly entertain the possibility that religions in general may be described in this fashion, so stubbornly do they resist analysis and decision.

There exists, then, a third authority that binds traditional metaphysics together with metanomics, as I call it, the principles of which remain to be elaborated, associating the intellect with the emotions, culture with nature; more precisely, the two metas link up with the subjective (reason and heart, abstractions and sentiments) both the objective (the inert and living worlds beneath heaven) and the collective (you and me) without excluding the emotive. Looked at in this way, it finally becomes clear why the Greeks used the same word, *nomos*, for the laws of nature and the laws of human society.

The house thus built, today still only imagined, would therefore be all-encompassing, surpassing our comprehension, since the abstract and the rational are intermingled in it with the emotions, with social life, with crystal, with the

floral and the bestial, at dawn and at sunset—the list goes
on without end.

But religion does not only designate, for the faithful,
those relations that unite us with God, and, for unbelievers, the relations that we have with those who are similar to
us and those who are different—the axes that I have called
vertical and horizontal, respectively; it also designates *the
relation as such*, relations in general, the total set of possible
relations, in respect of cognition as well as the various and
many things there are to be known. Through the indefinite
integral of the web it has spun, religion puts us in the world;
we are in the world through this integral.

Curiously, cognitive science does not have a word to designate this global subjective function. It is innate in human
beings. But has it ever really been explored? Its object is
the religious domain, for which this function serves as its
subject, as well as the objective domain that it seeks to apprehend. With regard to a totalizing function of this kind,
the religious domain includes the stars and human beings,
the creation and end of the world, our destiny, collective
and individual, time and history, the small flowers and the
grass of the fields, the wolves, birds, and lambs, physics and
morality, justice and law, medicine and health, sexuality, and
who knows what else—the totality of what exists, actually
and potentially. What escapes its grasp? Nothing. If religion
binds together all the functions usually considered to be
cognitive, these functions jointly seek to apprehend human
beings and all the things of the world, without exception,
bound together. If that seems contrary to all reason and beyond all emotion, it has always been thus for human beings,
since their beginning and down through the generations and
centuries, over the whole of the terraqueous surface of the

globe; just as culture cannot be known without music, so too it cannot be known without religion. Religion, aptly named, is the universal *binder*; the divine is this *binding*.

Two Accounts

In a single bound, stunning and fairly recent, the sciences have joined this process of integration. The grand narrative that they are constructing together covers the same span as what may be called sacred history. The week recounted in Genesis is better explained by the Big Bang, the cooling of the universe, the formation of planetary systems, including our own, the advent of living creatures; the Flood corresponds to variations in climate and associated marine transgressions; the appearance of mankind before the Paleolithic locates it in the paradise of gatherers; Abel and Cain figuratively express the invention of agriculture and animal breeding in the Neolithic; the Tower of Babel naively depicts the dispersion of cultures and languages. Abraham appeared in the axial age. The remarkable story of the aboriginal races of Australia, having arrived there by taking advantage of receding waters, only then to be trapped by their return, puts one in mind of the crossing of the Red Sea by the Hebrew people, who profited first from its drying up and then from the swallowing up of their pursuers when the waters rushed in again. The Tables of the Law received by Moses prefigured the invention of legislation and the inscription of the Twelve Tables in Rome. And so on.

In spite of their obvious differences, each of these parallel accounts records the imagination's advance toward the truth. Just as politics distinguishes between temporal and spiritual power, so too we have here, on the one hand, the heaviness of reality and the weight of truth, and, on the other, the lightness of images filled with hope. Just so, a *structural analogy* between the two relates a single adventure, a single odyssey, a single duration, worldwide and human. When we consider its successive stages in isolation, it is difficult to detect a unified pattern; and yet, when we take a broader view, it is readily apparent. Between the sciences and religion we now encounter a new synthesis, a new connection between the sacred and the secular, an unexpected northwest passage.

Formerly, and until quite recently, these two authorities fought over specific, analytically distinct issues, such as the earth's rotation and the evolution of living species. To the undeniable local victories of the one there now corresponds today, in this moment of synthesis, a strange global peace that has yet to be illuminated.

Beyond this correspondence, still wholly formal, beyond even the third authority, the cognitive function that desires and seeks it, we must try to characterize the power that brings the complementary narratives together. What dynamism can account for the stunning structural analogy that connects them?

The Risk of Fundamentalism
As a totality has no exterior, and is therefore potentially totalitarian, it quickly becomes exclusionary and punitive. I know everything, I have an answer for every question, I have a solution for every problem: all is revealed by my light. Therefore they do not exist, those who do not participate in the global integration function—not the function as such, whose manner of operation is for the moment unknown, but the dominant opinion from which they dissent, the party line they refuse to accept. Through the very realization of this totalitarian potential, dogmatic minds in positions of power

claim for themselves the right of life and death over those who do not share their views. Whence the wars, crimes, and exactions, so frequent in the history of religions and still so painful in our own time; whence the hideous lie of killing in the name of justice, inflicting pain in the name of compassion, torturing in the name of mercy.

The entire habitable world, our common home, risks becoming a prison from which no one is allowed to escape, like a blockhouse patrolled by gunners who shoot on sight and kill strangers, rather than an ordinary house, or a yurt, an igloo, a wigwam, a teepee, or a villa, equipped with doors through which all people can enter and windows that open to let in the air, a convivial inn welcoming tired and sometimes anxious travelers, also vacationers.

In choosing between the freedom to enter and leave our global dwelling, as we please, and the obligation to remain there, in involuntary confinement, we are forced to accept the fact that each religion must live with uncertainty as to how it will develop over time. In other words: either doubt is consubstantial with faith, each one an aspect of some larger function, just as inhalation and exhalation jointly constitute breathing, or it is expelled by dogmatic certainty, blind to the obviousness of undecidability.

History of Science

Doubt brings about a progressive loss of integration and, with it, violence. Yet science, throughout its history, in continually working to weaken the claims of religion, has brought about a gradual appreciation of their intimate and virtual connection. Christianity in its various denominations seems to me revelatory in this regard. Confronted with new discoveries, concerning the motion of the earth, for example, or the evolution of species, the Catholic Church was forced to reconsider its own teachings, and in this way, slowly, came to abandon dogmatism. While retaining their global ambition, Christian authors began to incorporate historical, symbolic, or relative interpretations, for no one could any longer defend the earth's immobility, or ignore the existence of fossils and the evidence of evolution they furnished. In freeing itself from dogma, Christianity discovered, little by little, that the doctrine of nonviolence, so far from being a weakness, was actually its greatest strength. We have never properly appreciated the enormous benefit that was derived from these repeated battles with scientific explanation, in-variably ending in defeat. The power of temporal truths purified Christianity and led it to embrace its true nature: the spiritual.

Religions that did not do this, that did not step back, reconsider, filter, that did not lighten, soften, weaken, went on insisting on incontrovertible truths and continued to seek temporal power. Hardened, they continued to kill in the name of a global truth, contestable and, in any case, undecidable.

I have compared sacred history with the grand narrative related by the sciences. It must never be forgotten, however, that, in the matter of violence, the sciences, for their part, bear responsibility for the special horror of Nagasaki.

Violence Is Radical Evil
The abuses for which religions are responsible bring us to the heart of the problem. Violence, the evil spawn of human relations, begotten by killing on an individual and on a mass scale, spread by disease, parasites, and microbes, by old age and pain, by water, earth, air, fire, by floods, seismic shocks,

tornados, fires—violence, the dark side of energy, universally dominates us.

For a long time we associated these things. The mortal, religious violence done to Iphigenia in exchange for the physical violence of the wind that carried Agamemnon onward to the sociopolitical violence of war; the violence done to Jephthah's daughter, similarly put to death as the price of a victory. Oedipus, king of Thebes, suffered for the plague that ravaged his city; sailors threw Jonah into the sea in order to appease the rage of the winds; the earth quaked with Christ's dying breath.

In the meantime the habit of analysis has led us to separate these things. It has allowed us to study the various aspects of violence, and sometimes, happily, a consequence of the search for truth, to contain it. I bring these aspects together, in order to try to understand the profound dynamic that causes them all to flourish. Or so it may appear. I am not actually the one who brings them together. In reality, it is *violence itself, extreme evil, that brings them together.* Why? Because violence is first and foremost a form of energy: the energy of waves and flames, of animals and plants, of men and women; the energy of enthusiasm and suffering, creative impulses both. Violence is an energy, a motive force; but its nature is capable of being modified, just as the direction of a boat can be altered by manipulating its rudder.

Energy

Science, social organization, personal behaviors, religious rites, and cultural practices generally were born, I believe, of the experience of violence, of the terror it engenders, of the measures that were taken to alleviate it, soften it, avoid it, and, if possible, to master it. With a firm hand on the rudder, we set a course, channeling the power of violence, which becomes harmful or useful depending on the angle of the rudder blade. What can we do to make sure that it will be useful?

All violence depends on energy, neutral in and of itself. It may assume the form of murder, or the fury of a tornado, but it can sometimes be oriented in a less dangerous direction. As René Girard has convincingly argued, collective violence, diffuse to begin with, comes to be focused and concentrated on the head of a single person, the scapegoat. In this way its energy is channeled in another direction. Everything of a constructive nature that human beings have succeeded in making and doing is a consequence of tactics and strategies that have been devised to bring about this diversion. For the direction and point of application of the energy of violence *can* be changed. The hope of making this very real possibility a reality is the driving force of human history; it has made the world in which we live today.

We are left with a series of questions. What path has this energy followed until now, what path will it follow in the future? To what extent can we divert its course when it threatens to take an evil turn? Can we tell exactly when it will begin to drift in the wrong direction? No doubt we will have to go back to its origin, to its first and smallest manifestation, before it finally overwhelms us, before we are no longer able, in our weakness, to control it. We must locate the point at which Lucretius's atoms begin unpredictably to swerve—the *clinamen*!

Examples

The sciences seek to account for the enormous power of the things of the world, occasionally in order to subordinate it to therapeutic and other benign ends. Politics exploits human

violence, morality tries to combat it, religion aims at sublimating it. These four cultural practices—scientific, political,
ethical, and religious, all of them energetic practices—are
concerned with the energy deployed by violence, with its
fatal orientation. So it is in the case of law and tragic theater,
also the media, faithful servants and auxiliaries of its ravages,
which speak of nothing but violence; also sports, let us not
forget sports.

Method

How can hatred be transformed in each of us into creative
energy, aggressiveness into benevolence? Collectively, how
can we transform hurricanes into windmills, redirect floods
into canals and irrigation reservoirs, convert perpetual wars
into lasting peace and religious conflicts into mystic ecstasies? How can we divert violence toward other ends, while
preserving its energy and placing it in the service of action,
cognition, social organization, and ecstasy, and in this way,
as Péguy put it, go from the political to the mystical?

These great works, these journeys, pilgrimages, stations
of the cross, crossings of the desert, methods—thus the hard
and unending labor of all cultures. A book falling under
the head of metanomics could begin by describing these
journeys, successful and failed alike, the transmutations that
have inspired scholarly discoveries, masterworks of painting,
sublime musical compositions, charitable gifts, peace of the
sort that is rarely found among peoples—forms of mysticity,
one and all.

Rather to my surprise, I find that I have been meditat-
ing in this book, from the very beginning, on the power of
things, both real and virtual: hot spots, explosions within

cathedrals, funereal spectacles, resurrection, and so on. Read
it as a treatise on energy—the energy deployed by violence.

Failure, Waste, Entropy
We are well aware of the ingenuity that the sciences are
capable of, and while we profit from their triumphal applications, we are aware, too, that ingenuity can degenerate into
tragedy, on both a local and a global scale—Hiroshima, on
the one hand, and, on the other, rampant pollution that destroys living creatures and, little by little, the planet itself. We
have learned from Machiavelli, and still more from the *Iliad*,
where political violence leads; and while we have learned to
appreciate the alternative held out by the search for peace, we
know, too, that it can lead instead to tyrannical regimes and
brutal wars. We practice morality, not always successfully, it
is true; but sometimes we are able to transform our cruelty
and aggression, our original sin, into creative action. As for
religion, it traces the path that I have tried to follow in this
book, though sometimes it deteriorates into sectarian conflict
and the persecution of heretics.

Strangely, these four domains—science, politics, ethics,
and religion—resemble one another. Sublimating energy,
attenuating violence is in some sense their common purpose;
when it is achieved, there nonetheless remain residual and
invariant traces of this violence, this authentic and primal
sin, always present, active, devouring. Satan fights, obstructs,
contradicts; he ignores peace.

Thus the sciences navigate between the informative and
luminous formalities of mathematics and the comforts derived from technology, on the one hand, and, on the other,
the catastrophe of Nagasaki; politics wavers between the spiritual and the temporal; ethics aspires to benevolence, but falls

into hypocrisy. And what are we to say about the relationship between the Wars of Religion and the gentle ecstasy of mysticism? Soft the end sought; hard the waste born of failure.

Similarly, energy drifts toward entropy; only very rarely does it furnish negentropy and information. The gradual and fatal drift by which energy descends into entropy weaves the threads, spins the web of our short life; more rarely still, whatever small amount of negentropy it may yield enables us, in intensely brief moments of time, to think—ideally, to invent.

Fires

In the best case, as I say, transmutations of energy lead from violence, dark energy, to peace, a creative force. Heraclitus invited visitors to warm themselves before the fire of his kitchen oven, saying that here were gods too, no less than in the fire of Hestia's hearth. On the morning of Pentecost, the Holy Ghost descended upon the apostles in tongues of fire; when they then began speaking in tongues, the motley crowd that gathered was filled with amazement, "because everyone heard them speak in his own language" (Acts 2:3–6); thus fire led on to universal understanding. These two stories, short and dense, cognitive and religious, at all events energetic, bear constant rereading. They sum up what I have been trying to show in this book, namely, the connection between fire, which is to say energy, and the religious domain; also between energy and various cultural practices.

Plato imagined flames of a similar sort to burn in the darkness of a cave, behind a group of prisoners, who, on being freed, emerged from the illusory shadows of the cave's wall into broad daylight, the dazzling light of the truth—symbolizing, of course, the passage from ignorance to knowledge, but also, more concretely, from the burning to the luminous. Descartes put himself inside a stove, whose energy burned and heated; he began increasingly to doubt and to struggle against an evil genius who strongly resembles Satan, until finally discovering a personal truth guaranteed by God himself. So, too, we have been able to understand the process by which the primordial hearth of the Big Bang condensed an infinite energy, through a cosmology that has practical applications in our own small world.

What difference is there between these various journeys of the mind and the pilgrimages of Saint John of the Cross, crossing the dark night before discovering mystic ecstasy at the summit of Mount Carmel? And the ecstasy of Saint Francis of Assisi, in whom miserable nakedness culminated in perfect joy? One finds the same transfer between burning and light: the words "divine" and "luminous," having the same Greco-Latin root, go hand in hand. I even wonder sometimes whether the course of history as Hegel and Marx imagined it, which reproduces the theology of Joachim of Fiore—Hegel's idea of "negative" activity, the journey to absolute knowledge with its many trials of self-examination; Marx's concept of class struggle and dialectic, mimicking the dynamic Joachim identified while altering it so that the dream of a classless society guaranteed by the reign of the spirit will one day be realized—did not obey the same schema, the climbing of Calvary, the descent from it, and the resurrection that followed. From the auto-da-fés of the Inquisition to the reign of the Enlightenment, from the cruel flame of the false to the divine clarity of the truth . . .

Just as religion can lapse into the exploitation of indulgences and the sentencing to death of heretics, so too fundamental scientific research, often supervised by academic administrators who know nothing about it, tends today to be less concerned with advancing the cause of knowledge than with landing government contracts for the purpose of making money for a sponsoring institution. With the cooptation of science by financial interests, the obsession with profits and glory drives a wedge between research and the truth. To prevent the vertical from falling into the horizontal, the biblical prophets sought to liberate the Hebrew people from their false gods; holy purity extinguished the flames of the sacred; science, condemned as bourgeois but nonetheless true, supplanted Michurin and Lysenko, buffoons anointed as authorities by Soviet ideology.

The scientific community, numerous and dense, exists only thanks to inventors, who are very rare. The religious community, likewise numerous and dense, exists only thanks to mystics, no less rare. Politics is doomed, by its nature and function, to the unhappy fate of not being able to free itself from the horizontal plane, where violence eternally recurs.

The Scapegoat
Girard's theory of social violence perfectly describes the development of this dynamic in a sacred context. Violence, always latent, explodes at a moment of crisis and comes to be resolved with the lynching of a scapegoat. This murder succeeds only in postponing a lasting solution to the problem, however, since once peace has been reestablished, violence will break out again at the next opportunity, the next time a critical moment occurs, with the result that it is endlessly recycled throughout the immanent horizontal plane where groups are forged. Alas, no victim, not even Christ, is the last one to die. Because the Messiah died in order to wash away *all the sins of the world*, he ought to have been the last person sentenced to death in a world henceforth purged of

violence; thus he said, "Get behind me, Satan!" And yet we know of no individual, no group, no nation since Good Friday that has never made war, never put innocent persons to death, persecuted minorities, tormented and raped children and women.

Girard's schema, as true as it is universal in space and constant throughout history, ceaselessly reproduces itself, like systole and diastole. Malign violence is propagated like a wave: in its distributive aspect, it is localized; localized, it is redistributed and once again becomes localized. Like the roaring lion of I Peter 5:8, it prowls about seeking whom it may devour: *tanquam leo rugiens circuit quaerens quem devoret.* It moves circuitously, which is to say in a circle, in an eternal return. Will we ever be delivered from it? Psalm 90, sung at night prayer, compline, the last canonical hour of the day, vividly describes this perennial combat, which must be resumed every evening, as much in one's innermost soul as in and through social intercourse.

Onward

Now we begin our arduous journey on the steep road toward holiness, in the hope of leaving the teeth of lions behind, once and for all. A painting by Carpaccio, one of a cycle of nine panels that hang in the Scuola di San Giorgio degli Schiavoni, in Venice, shows Saint Jerome entering the grounds of a monastery, followed by a lion he has tamed, which nonetheless so frightens the monks there that they flee in a furious swirl of robes. We must do away with malice while preserving its force, redirecting it to serve benign purposes.

In speaking of the plane of horizontal immanence where violence roams and of the vertical volume where peace reigns, I cannot help but regret that psychoanalysts have appropriated the term "sublimation," for if it could be stripped of its pathological connotations it would describe exactly what the passage from the one to the other involves.

Freed Slaves

I have tried elsewhere to show that three of the pictures by Carpaccio in the Scuola di San Giorgio represent this very same road. First one comes to the dragon trampling the bones of its victims; next, the tamed lion; finally, the lovable small dog wondering at Saint Augustine in ecstasy in his study. Three beasts: wild, trained, domesticated. Always the same path, tortuous, arduous, between the fire of combat and the spirituality of prayer, passing through the taming of ferocity. How does one climb up to the summit of this holy and peaceable mountain, described by the prophet, where the lion lies down with the lamb? The lion and the serpent you will trample underfoot: *conculcabis leonem et draconem* (Psalm 91:13). Alas, the spirit of combat, however heroic, however glorified, spreads throughout a group and becomes concentrated on a victim, perpetuating the very violence it seeks to bring to an end. Whether one fights on the side of the angel or the beast, in equal numbers or not, everyone fights. No, do not see this as a conflict between good and evil, for both sides *do* evil. Whether the battle is all against all, or all against one, everyone *does* evil. Appeasement consists in never putting one's hand on the sword. To him who strikes you on the cheek, offer the other one also.

This long journey of *conversion*, from the angry flames of hell to the serene lights of heaven, does not differ from the one that Dante recounted in the *Divine Comedy*. One of the many profound insights of this magnificent work cruelly illuminates the author's own experience, as he frankly acknowledges; but it was also the experience of the pilgrim of his tale. Are they the same person? I do not know, for here we are faced with an unfathomable difference, between the one who speaks, who relates, and who sometimes advises, and the one who travels *along the same route*, courageously, and who often stumbles. Understanding more, understanding better does not advance the pilgrim's progress by an inch. When I said in my book on Jules Verne that this journey resembles an exodus more than a method, I did not yet have in mind the biblical text relating the Hebrew people's escape from slavery in Egypt and the crossing of the desert before arriving finally in the promised land. Sterile, arid, the desert reminds us of a place where all energy, life-giving or otherwise, is nullified. The Book of Exodus forcefully reminds us of the difference between someone who merely looks at a map and someone, suffering from terrible thirst, who actually trudges through the desert represented by the map. On the mountain, God tells Moses that he will show him the way and the land of Canaan—and also that he will never reach it.

To put it another way: Dante describes Purgatory as the kingdom of the mind, only a stage, limited to apprehension by the intellect. Only by means of a metamorphosis can it be gone beyond. A perilous leap, a death, a resurrection? In drawing up a map of the journey, I can indefinitely multiply subtle analyses that delight reason and the understanding— and after that, I keep on asking myself, what comes next? Afterward I will not be any closer to my goal. The intellect boasts of its brilliance in immanence; but it is of no help whatever in attaining transcendence, by means of a passage, whether through sieve, saddle, or strait, that by itself, iso- lated, it cannot find. It remains trapped in Purgatory. My knowledge is only a purgative.

Pascal, in distinguishing the orders of the mind and of
charity, classifying them one after the other, differentiating
them with infinite precision, arrived at a similar conclusion.
Even the prince of savants, Archimedes himself, did not attain the order of Jesus Christ. Saint Anselm spoke of *fides
quaerens intellectum*, faith seeking understanding, the easi-
est of all quests; but understanding seeking faith, there lies
an immense undertaking, a road that is both blocked and
without end.

The Definitive Obstacle

Girard rightly saw sacrificial behavior as an attempt to arrest
the spread of violence. But this solution, though it is universal and constant, remains, as I have said, periodic. The lion
will reawaken. But I do not have, we do not have any idea of
how to stop it once and for all; no doubt there is no solution.
The image of Carpaccio's *Saint Jerome and the Lion* is both
convenient and naïve, and in any case of no practical value.
The real lion will never be tamed; it will endlessly go on roaring, go on seeking someone, something to devour. This is
the obstacle encountered over and over again in the course
of the journey: the wall, the lack, the unbridgeable abyss.

Now, it is on just this lack, this bottomless well, this
puteal, this hot spot, this empty tomb that the axis of transcendence is erected, raised up. The vertical is planted in,
driven into the hole of the horizontal. In supplementing the
cycle of the Passion, of death and hatred, by the miracle of
the Resurrection, it may be that Christ pointed to this high
road. For there must be at least a boundless, infinite God
who can help us to cross this abyss, this absence of any individual, collective, human solution, on the horizontal plane
of immanence; who can enable us to solve the problem of

persistent, unending, indefinite violence. A God of wrath and vengeance could only perpetuate it; only a God of love could eradicate it once and for all, forever.

God, deliver *us* from evil. Deliverance, collective and political, having not yet occurred, this invocation remains a prayer, a supplication, a fervent hope that a way forward may yet be found. Is it nonetheless possible to imagine that individuals may be exonerated from this violence? By all means. Saintliness may rightly be defined as just this state of deliverance from evil, a state of being that opens a new life, a life of deeds, sentiments, and thoughts that are always benignly energetic, never evil or maliciously motivated. Saints propagate peace. Because they are many, we may hope that they will finally usher in a new era of history, a new humanity. In mystic ecstasy, active in all religions, and therefore universal, the presence of God and of the divine will fill to overflowing those who experience it with a sovereign joy, perfect, peaceable, safe from all evil, gracious.

Agen 1945

Vincennes 2019

INDEX

Hallyday, Johnny (Jean-Philippe
  Léo Smet), 101, 149
Hegel, Georg Wilhelm Friedrich,
  70, 129, 185
Heraclitus, 184
Hermes, 116, 173
Herod, 31–32, 131
Hippasus of Metapontum, 9,
  66
Hippocrates, 15
Hiroshima and Nagasaki, 10, 31,
  33–35, 179, 183
historiography, hypercritical,
  26–27
history, philosophy of, 68–70. *See
  also* time and tempo
Hitler, Adolf, 150
Hobbes, Thomas, 121
Holy Family, 131–34
homosexual marriage, 134
Horatius (Publius Horatius
  Cocles), 82–83
hot spots: abyss and, 47, 190;
  art, 38–39; cathedrals, 44;
  convergence on the present,
  55–56; defined, 4–5; of ego,
  37–38; Eucharist, 66; Galileo,
  mathematical physics, and Incarnation, 10–12; Hiroshima,
  33–35; Incarnation and vertical-
  horizontal intersection, 75; line
  of, 62–63; Midas and Gyges,
  13–15; money, mathematics,
  and alphabet, 14–19; physical
  records of, 117; religious axial
  age, 17–18; *sicut* and, 71–72;
  subjective and collective, 36;
  sundial, 6–7; the Three Wise
  Men and Epiphany, 19–26, 32–
  33; trajectory of, 54–55

Hugo, Victor, 106
human sacrifice, 117–18

image: media and, 98–105; virtual
  world and, 97–98
Immaculate Conception, 137–40
Incarnation, 11–12, 41, 51, 75, 148
incense, 20–21
information: digital, 19; energy
  and, 7, 9–10, 16, 25, 28; entropy and, 28; sundial and
  pyramid as *gnomonic*, 7–8
Iphigenia, 118, 180
Isaac, 6
Islam, 52

Jacob, 6
Jaspers, Karl, 17
Jephthah, 117–18, 180
Jeremiah, 38–39, 87–88
Jerome, Saint, 187
Jesus Christ: calming the storm
  at sea, 120–21; as country
  dweller or homeless, 106–10,
  112; failure to recognize, 142–
  45; flight to Egypt, 74; Joseph
  and, 131, 133; Magi, Epiphany,
  and, 21–26; night and birth of,
  72–74; pardon for sin, 87–88;
  Passion, 37, 40, 77, 81, 88–89,
  122–23, 190; Peter's denial of,
  76–81; praising, 152–53; Resurrection of, 141–49; Samaritan
  woman at the well and, 6, 129;
  temptation of, 87; Transfiguration, 36–37; as virtual, 147. *See
  also* Incarnation
Joachim, Saint, 138–39
Joachim of Fiore (Gioacchino da
  Fiore), 69–70, 71, 185

CPSIA information can be obtained
at www.ICGtesting.com
Printed in the USA
JSHW030152100222
22734JS00003B/5

9 781503 631496